THE PROBLEM OF VALUES IN EDUCATIONAL THOUGHT

The Problem of Values
in Educational Thought

PHILIP L. SMITH

IOWA STATE UNIVERSITY PRESS / AMES

87-304

PHILIP L. SMITH is associate professor of Philosophy of Education, Ohio State University. Besides this book, he is author of *Sources of Progressive Thought in American Education* (1980), an intellectual history of progressive educational theory.

© 1982 The Iowa State University Press. All rights reserved

Printed by The Iowa State University Press, Ames, Iowa 50010

First edition, 1982

Library of Congress Cataloging in Publication Data

Smith, Philip L.
    The problem of values in educational thought.

    Includes index.
    1. Smith, Philip L.   2. Education—Philosophy.
3. Judgement.   I. Title.
LB885.S5717   370′.1   81–23650
ISBN 0-8138-1853-2   AACR2

Publication of this work has been made possible in part by a grant from the Andrew W. Mellon Foundation.

ALEXANDER

T O   ADAM

ADRIENNE

C O N T E N T S

PREFACE   ix

1 Patterns of Educational Thought   3
      The Genesis of Theory   3
      Theory as an Idea   4
      Realism and Instrumentalism   5
      Theories in Education   9

2 The Logic of Justification   13
      Justifications as Arguments   13
      Three Types of Arguments: Proofs,
          Explanations, Justifications   16

3 Creating and Using Standards   27
      Descriptive and Prescriptive Propositions   27
      Bewildering Cases   28
      Brute Facts and Institutional Facts   31
      Regulative Rules and Constitutive Rules   33
      Justifications and Proofs   36
      Facts and Values   38

4 Intuitionism as a Theory of Value:
          A Concession to Formalism   41
      Criticisms of Intuitionism   45

5 Emotivism as a Theory of Value:
          The Extremes of Nominalism   49
      Criticisms of Emotivism   56

6 Prescriptivism as a Theory of Value:
      An Amendment to Emotivism   63
      Criticisms of Prescriptivism   68
      Rationality as a Logical Stipulation   70

7 Justifying Judgments of Value:
      A Fourth Reply Revisited   75
      Definitions of Value   77
      Deflating the Naturalistic Fallacy   77
      Confronting the Is/Ought Dilemma   79
      Naturalism as a Theory of Value   82

INDEX   87

P R E F A C E

This book focuses on the origin and nature of values in educational thought, a philosophical inquiry which, as an aspect of social and political theory, motivates as many questions about values as one can imagine. These questions are by no means limited to education, however; they are perennial and they apply to every important aspect of human life.

I have never ceased to be amazed at the extent to which people can disagree, often with great passion, over what does or does not have value. Even more surprising is how strongly they can disagree, also often with great passion, over what is or should be subject to normative debate, the kind of disputation that examines the value or worth of things.

After many years and much thought, this book is the result of my efforts to come to terms with these puzzlements. I do not for a moment regard its conclusions as the final word, nor do I mean to suggest that in every case what I have said has never been said before. I have tried to make the issue of values clear as a philosophical problem and to assemble a set of ideas, some of which are my own, that might help in solving this problem. Whether I have succeeded is better left for others to judge, but I must admit to a certain sense of satisfaction that makes me want to forge ahead and build upon this writing as a foundation. Time will tell if my feeling is presumptuous.

I thank <u>Educational Theory</u>, © Copyright Board of Trustees, University of Illinois, for their permission

to reprint in Chapter 3 material from one of my articles
that appeared in Volume 28, Number 1 (Winter 1978).

I also acknowledge my gratitude to the many
colleagues and students who have, in one way or another,
assisted me. Joseph O'Rourke, Edgar Dale, Jack Holton,
and Bill Taylor strived valiantly to help me find the
right words, and Bill Zornes worked hard on the Index.
Most of all, I am indebted to Betty Chapin, whose patience
can never be adequately repaid. She not only assisted
in my writing, but helped me to think more clearly and,
generally, created an atmosphere in which I could work.

PLS

Columbus, Ohio

THE PROBLEM OF VALUES IN EDUCATIONAL THOUGHT

CHAPTER 1

PATTERNS OF EDUCATIONAL THOUGHT

The aim of education is deceivingly simple: to foster the capacities for intelligent practical action, or what might alternatively be called "enlightened conduct." The means for achieving this aim are equally obvious. Since we cannot assume that the educational process is natural or inevitable, we must somehow intervene in the activities of those being educated. Nonetheless, while most educators have at least an intuitive understanding of this aim, and while many educators have a knack for using the guideposts of common sense when it comes to the selection of means, neither intuition nor common sense are always sufficient for dealing effectively with educational problems.

THE GENESIS OF THEORY

So long as the results of our labors tally with our expectations there is little incentive for reflection. We think only when we have a need and we theorize only when we have a need to think consistently and systematically. The hunter who can bag his prey easily has no motive for speculation. And the farmer who can grow his crops without difficulty has no use for theories about farming. Theories take on meaning only in a problematic context. Where nothing is perplexing or indecisive, when action is free and uninhibited, theory, like all things intellectual, will appear conspicuously out of place. However, where there is conflict, when the situation is confused, unsettled, or disturbed, even the hunter and the farmer will be theoretically inclined.

3

For precisely this reason--uncertainty of action --educators are frequently attracted to abstract ideas. A serious-minded practitioner is quick to realize that educational situations are extremely complex and constantly subject to change. Without perspective and sense of direction, which only theories can provide, success in achieving even the most limited objective can be nearly impossible. Moreover, a theoretical orientation can be helpful when educational principles are being challenged or when they no longer seem appropriate. Where educational disputes center on ideas, and not merely on the application of ideas, we need, in addition to the perspective and sense of direction that can help us reach our goals, the capacity to justify our goals, to conceive and evaluate them clearly, and, of course, to change them when reason demands.

THEORY AS AN IDEA

A theory can be a means of reconstructing a disturbed situation. But, applied more basically, it can be a source of meaning, a way of making sense out of non-sense. By itself experience tells us little. Without ideas to interpret what we see, everything appears as brute fact, as a succession of mere happenings. By providing us with a consistent and systematic set of ideas, theories enable us to organize our experience. We can see things as a series of more or less meaningful events, meaningful in themselves as well as in relation to other events. More is involved here than simple description. In a sense we create what we see by constructing our experiences symbolically, by ideas. When these ideas work together they operate as a theory, itself a symbolic construction, that shapes our experience on an even larger scale. We learn _from_ experience; not merely _by_ experience; we take thought about what there is _to_ be learned and experience things vicariously without having to rely solely on brute sense perception.

By placing our knowledge in a consistent and systematic form, theories do more than provide for what early Positivist philosophers called "economy of thought" or "mental shorthand." The organization effected by a theory has the consequence of simplifying phenomena and creating a structure for the storage and retrieval of information. However, these effects are not fundamental. According to Abraham Kaplan they are the by-products of

a more basic function: "to make sense of what would
otherwise be inscrutable or unmeaning empirical findings.
A theory is more than a synopsis of the moves that have
been played in the game of nature; it also sets forth
some idea of the rules of the game, by which the moves
become intelligible."[1]   We can say that for precisely
this reason theories attest to truth as well as provide
for meaning. As Kaplan points out: "A hypothesis may
be as much confirmed by fitting it into a theory as by
fitting it to the facts. For it then enjoys the support
provided by the evidence for all the other hypotheses
of that theory."[2]

REALISM AND INSTRUMENTALISM
     The traditional view of inquiry regards a theory
as a picture or map. This conception was especially
popular in the eighteenth and nineteenth centuries when
scientific researchers believed they were discovering
the world in the same manner as explorers. Advancements
were thought to be a matter of extending the range of
our understanding. Of course, details would have to be
filled in, but significant progress was assumed possible
only at the frontiers of knowledge. As Kaplan depicts
this view: "Once a territory is discovered and mapped,
we plant our flag on it, and it is ours forever."[3]
Knowledge is thought to grow by extension; a relatively
full explanation of a small region is carried over to
an explanation of adjoining regions. And science is
conceived as "an edifice, a mosaic, an erector set, or
a jigsaw puzzle--and it is built up piece by piece."[4]
     In criticizing this view Kaplan rejects the idea
of a theory as a picture or map. He considers the implied
analogy to be dubious at best: "to make the territory
truly ours we must live on it, colonize and develop it;
thereby the face of the land will be changed, and new
maps will be called for."[5] A theory is an instrument
of action that reflects our choice in a problematic

---

1.   Abraham Kaplan, The Conduct of Inquiry (San Francisco:
     Chandler, 1964), p. 302.
2.   Ibid., p. 302.
3.   Ibid., p. 306.
4.   Ibid., p. 305.
5.   Ibid., p. 306.

situation. Instead of picturing or mapping reality, it
serves as a tool of inquiry. Chauncey Wright (1830-1875)
used to say that ideas are finders and not merely
summaries of truth.[6] Theories are not different in
this regard. They suggest, stimulate, and direct what
we do, not as a creed but as a policy. That theories
operate to connect apparently diverse phenomena is beyond
dispute. The point is that they do not achieve this end
by mental or symbolic replication of an antecedently
existing subject matter, but rather by prescribing conduct
that allows us to move about in accordance with our
intentions. "Properly speaking, instrumentalism is not
an alternative to the realist conception, but a
specification of what it means to picture reality. The
map is a device by which we can get from place to place;
its correspondence with the territory consists in the
fact that it can be so used."[7]

On the instrumentalist view, knowledge grows more
by intension than extension. Rather than beginning with
a full explanation of a small region and expanding it
to cover adjoining regions, growth by intension starts
with a partial explanation of an entire area and works
to make it more and more complete. This idea "is
associated with such metaphors for the scientific
enterprise as developing a photographic negative, bringing
binoculars to a sharper focus, or gradually illuminating
a darkened room--progress is not piecemeal but gradual
on a larger scale."[8] While it cannot be said that
instrumentalism repudiates the idea that knowledge grows
by extension, it does not assume that the facts speak
for themselves. The facts get their meaning from our
theories, and while new discoveries undoubtedly work to
change our ideas, new theories have the effect of
transforming what we have previously known.

Grover Maxwell is one of many who have objected to
instrumentalism on the grounds that it cannot explain
why a theory is successful, while realism "provides the

---

6. Gail Kennedy, "The Pragmatic Naturalism of Chauncey
    Wright," in Studies in the History of Ideas, Vol. 3,
    ed. the Department of Philosophy, Columbia University
    (New York: Columbia Univ. Press, 1935), pp. 477-506.
7. Kaplan, The Conduct of Inquiry, p. 306.
8. Ibid., p. 305.

very simple and cogent explanation that the entities referred to by well-confirmed theories exist."[9] Kaplan responded to this objection in two ways. First, "a scientifically significant explanation of the success of a theory is provided only by another theory, which makes clear the respect in which the earlier one did or failed to do justice to the data." To say that a theory works because it corresponds with reality may be "very simple and cogent," but it does not contribute much to our understanding. Second, and more importantly, however, is that instrumentalism is not forced to reject this view. "It emphasizes only that our reasons for affirming the existence of the entities in question often consist precisely in the fact that the theory referring to them is a successful one. The map is a good one because that is the shape of the territory, but we may have found that the territory has that shape in the course of making the map."[10]

Instrumentalism is opposed to the idea--often attributed to Francis Bacon (1561-1626)--that inquiry proceeds by surveying the "facts" until the laws that govern them are revealed. Then and only then can we organize these laws into a general and comprehensive theory. At times, however, even Bacon seemed to waver in this view. He thought of the scientist as neither wholly speculative--like a spider spinning his web from his own substance--nor wholly empirical--like an ant collecting data into a heap. He viewed the scientist more like a bee gathering and feeding on nectar, digesting it, and thereby transmuting it into the purest honey. Despite this declaration Bacon and his followers generally were inclined toward the ant. Perhaps this resulted as an overreaction to the excessive web-spinning of most continental Rationalists. But the fact remains that Realists have never accepted, or even understood, the broad conception of empiricism that is so essential for instrumentalism. Theirs is a very narrow empiricism.

---

9. Grover Maxwell, "The Ontological Status of Theoretical Entities," in Minnesota Studies in the Philosophy of Science, Vol. 3, ed. Herbert Feigl and Grover Maxwell (Minneapolis: Univ. of Minnesota Press, 1962), p. 22.
10. Kaplan, The Conduct of Inquiry, p. 307.

Experience is understood in terms that make positivism
unavoidable and, thus, ideas like that of instrumentalism
are regarded as meaningless.

However this may be, Instrumentalists believe that
theories have a creative dimension. That is to say, the
creative imagination plays a part in the process of theory
formation and is therefore involved in the context of
discovery. But it is also a factor in defining the theory
as a product and in creating its object, and so it enters
into the context of justification. A theory does not
just discover the facts; it is a way of looking at the
facts, of organizing and representing them, and to this
extent at least, of inventing or constructing them.
Kaplan makes reference to a class of puzzles that arise
as a result of the difficulty in understanding the variety
of ways in which experienced facts might be represented:

> The next number in the sequence 4, 14, 34, 42, . . .
> is 59; these are the express stops on the Eighth
> Avenue subway, as every New Yorker will tell you--if
> he thinks of it. The next letter in the sequence
> O, T, T, F, F, . . . is S; these are the initial
> letters of the number words "one," "two," "three,"
> . . . . We have been tricked because we were looking
> for properties of the thing-in-itself, and not of
> something constituted by the forms of the knowing
> mind. Freeing ourselves from the illusion that
> knowledge is only the apprehension of facts, quite
> independent of the mode of representation, is what
> Kant called the Copernican revolution. It is
> essential, I believe, to appreciating the role of
> scientific theory.[11]

Kaplan goes on to compare theoretical statements
and metaphors. A metaphor, he says, is of our own making:

> yet some metaphors are well-grounded and
> illuminating, while others are forced and contrived.
> Whether a metaphor is of the one sort or the other
> depends on the actual characteristics of what it
> is being applied to, but not in the relatively simple
> and straightforward way that marks the truth or
> falsehood of a literal statement. We may say that

---

11. Ibid., p. 308.

a theory is grounded in the facts, . . . but that
it does not constitute a direct representation of
the facts.[12]

Instrumentalism should not be equated with those
views that value only expediency and technical
rationality. On the contrary, its aim is enlightened
conduct, a goal that demands total commitment to
intellectual powers and moral sensibilities. Neither
should it be confused with a strict positivism that limits
cognitive meaning to observation statements. From this
perspective theories do no more than serve as signs for
concrete occurrences. But according to instrumentalism,
it may be that in a particular context of inquiry
observation statements are instrumental to the formation
of theories, rather than the other way around. Like
realism, it rejects the idea that theories are simply
means to other ends, especially when those ends have their
origins outside the context of inquiry. In Kaplan's
words: "they may also serve as ends in themselves--to
provide understanding, which may be prized for its own
sake. Only, to understand the world does not mean to
hold in our hands the blueprints by which God created
it, but very human sketches by which we ourselves can
find our way."[13]

THEORIES IN EDUCATION
Educational theories obviously contain elements from
such other fields as psychology, biology, and politics,
for example, but they remain distinctive by virtue of
their focus on the unique subject matter of education.
Wherever we can speak of such subject matter, we can speak
of theories pertaining to that subject matter. Not that
education is a discipline in some pure or narrow sense,
or that it constitutes an academic, as opposed to a
professional field of study, but it does represent an
area of human interest that cannot be fully defined or
reduced to more basic terms. That education does
represent an area of human interest is beyond debate.
That education cannot be fully defined or reduced to more
basic terms is a consequence of its nature as a human

12. Ibid., p. 309.
13. Ibid., p. 310.

institution. Like all human institutions, whether formalized or not, education is a reality in its own right. Whether conceived as a process or a product, it stands as a whole that is greater than the sum of its parts and, thus, it cannot be understood except as an entity.

Educational theories can also be described as answering important questions about education. That is, we need to know what to teach and how to teach effectively. We need to know who to teach, when to teach and where. Perhaps most importantly of all, we need to know why. No doubt this list could be extended. The point is that with the right theory we should never be at a loss for answers.

A theory is complete if it provides answers, at least implicitly, for all of the important questions relating to its subject matter; otherwise it is incomplete. If these answers are correct, the theory is sound; if not, it is unsound. In the case where the theory is either incomplete or unsound we may speak of it as flawed.

To say that educational theories are distinguishable by their subject matter is not to say that all efforts to deal with this subject matter are theoretical; it is merely to say that any theory that focuses on this subject matter is an educational theory. Likewise, to say that educational theories answer important questions about education is not to say that answers to these questions always have a basis in theory, but only that theories can provide us with a basis for answers. What makes a theory a theory is not so much its subject matter, or the questions it answers, but the type of understanding it provides. It organizes our experience and allows us to see things as a whole. From a logical point of view it represents a linguistic structure composed of three distinct elements: first, conceptions that define the theory's subject matter and the various ways in which it might be expressed; second, propositions or claims about that subject matter; and third, arguments designed to warrant those claims. In terms of logical priorities, conceptions precede propositions and propositions come before arguments. But in terms of those features that identify a theory as a theory we need to reverse these priorities. We could have any number of concepts and propositions and still not have a theory. A theory is designed to settle questions about its subject matter in a rational manner and, thus, requires the larger

context of argumentation. We can think of a theory as
a set of related arguments, implicit or explicit, intended
to rationally resolve the problems that arise in
connection with the substance of that theory.

Along these lines it is sometimes said that a theory
is an explanation and that "having a theory" means simply
"having an explanation." However, a theory always
involves more than a single explanation and, for that
matter, can never be restricted to one kind of argument.
On the first point, to equate a theory with an explanation
violates the conventional notion of a theory as defining
a context of meaning. A theory provides the framework
within which explanations are formulated and appraised; it
is not itself an explanation. An explanation is like
a hypothesis in this regard; although derived from a
theory it has a character all its own. On the second
point, while a theory supplies the basis for explanations,
it also establishes the foundation for proofs and
justifications. That is, with a theory we can explain
what might be otherwise inexplicable. Yet we can also
prove things in a logical or deductive sense, and justify
our judgments as warranted. Much should and will be said
about these various types of arguments. For now it is
sufficient to say that a theory incorporates all three
types: explanations, proofs, and justifications.

A theory is credible if it generates credible
arguments. But how can we tell if an argument is
credible? This question is undoubtedly a complicated
one and we should not pretend to answer it here. We need
only point out that while reliable arguments are always
difficult to construct, justifications present special
problems in this regard. Their purpose is to establish
the truth not merely in a logical or formal sense, as
in the case of proofs, but in a substantive sense where
the truth is assumed to have existential qualities, that
is to say, where it has reference to things outside the
argument itself. But justifications imply judgments and
judgments can never be established with certainty. The
skeptic always has grounds for rejecting a judgment and,
thus, for rejecting a justification. As applied to
judgments of fact this might not seem a serious
challenge. At least we have some idea of what it is we
are looking for and can defend our search as objective.
On the other hand, judgments of value give the impression
of being without any clear reference or basis in reality
for precisely the reason that values are exceedingly hard,

some would say impossible, to conceive. Were this
actually the case then justifications of value judgments
would be inherently irrational and the most we could hope
for is that justifications of factual judgments would
not eventually be shown to suffer from the same fatal
flaw.

    Of all the arguments that a theory might generate,
justifications of value judgments are in most respects
of the greatest importance. Not only do they focus on
the basic commitments of the theory, but usually they
represent issues that are matters of consequence in their
own right. If judgments of value are never justifiable
in the same manner as, say, judgments of fact, we will
be forced to admit that our theories always retain an
element of irrationality and that the problem of values
is likely to remain unresolved. The acceptance of any
theory would demand acceptance of its values as a matter
of pure faith. The only way to avoid this conclusion
is to show that normative arguments, arguments as to the
value or worth of things, have a logic similar to the
logic found in arguments that are not normative, and in
particular to factual arguments, a task to which we now
turn.

CHAPTER 2

THE LOGIC OF JUSTIFICATION

Of all the ideas found in rational disputation the idea of justification is the most likely to be used with thoughtless assurance. It plays such a central role in our writings and conversations that we hardly give it a second thought. The assumption appears to be that everyone knows perfectly well what "justification" means. None of us wants to look foolish, as surely we would if we disputed the obvious, so we continue as we always have, refusing to ponder the intricate windings of this seemingly simple conception.

But the question remains: How is this conception to be understood? We strive to justify an endless variety of things--actions, ideas, beliefs, attitudes, feelings, decisions, and principles are examples of this truism. Yet, despite their diversity of focus, justifications retain a number of defining characteristics. Not the least important is the fact that they can always be expressed in the form of propositions and ultimately in the form of an argument. Among other things this means they can be understood in rational terms, for, as linguistic constructions of reality, they presuppose a logical system that serves as a context for their formulation, analysis, and evaluation.

JUSTIFICATIONS AS ARGUMENTS

As a special kind of argument justifications display the features found in arguments generally. In the technical or formal sense, the term "argument" refers to an assumed relationship between ideas, or, more

accurately, between propositions. Within the context
of rational discourse it consists of a set of at least
two statements, one serving as a premise and the other
as a conclusion, where the conclusion is thought to follow
in some sense from the premise. Calling these statements
premise and conclusion does not imply that anyone actually
accepts them. Nor does it require that the conclusion
actually follows from the premise. It is merely to say
that these statements have specific functions within a
larger organization as components that can be analyzed
and evaluated as an argument.

Where the conclusion follows objectively from the
premise the argument is valid, otherwise it is invalid.
Validity means that one cannot rationally accept the
premise and reject the conclusion, that if the premise
is true (that is, it conforms to fact and/or agrees with
reason) the conclusion must also be true. But notice,
the premise need not be true, nor is it necessary for
anyone to believe that it is true. Insofar as validity
is concerned such considerations are beside the point.
We are asked merely to preface the premise with a
hypothetical phrase or subjunctive clause and to look
upon the conclusion as a consequence. Validity treats
truth lightly because truth is not really the issue.
The issue is whether there exists an organic or epistemic
relationship between the premise and conclusion of an
argument.

It would be well to explain here that an organic
relationship is one having a substantive basis in reality,
where the particulars of that reality are integral parts
of a larger structure or whole. An epistemic relationship
is one that allows us to acquire knowledge on the basis
of knowledge we already possess, where the knowledge we
already possess defines the necessary and sufficient
conditions for the knowledge we acquire or, saying the
same thing, where knowledge we already possess is
"epistemically basic" in its bearing on the knowledge
we acquire. It would be more in keeping with customary
language to describe the relationship between the premise
and conclusion of a valid argument as logical, necessary,
essential, or objective. But these expressions usually
remain general, ambiguous, and vague. Thus, the
preference for the terms "organic" and "epistemic" which
are more specific and precise.

To continue, if there does exist an organic or
epistemic relationship, then the argument is valid. If
there does not, then the argument is invalid. We can

demonstrate the validity of an argument by providing an explanation of the relationship between the premise and the conclusion. Often we can show this directly by supplying whatever information is needed to link the premise with the conclusion. On other occasions we can show this indirectly by taking the premise for granted and assuming the negation of the conclusion as a consequence. Does this produce a contradiction? If so, and if we can explain why, we can demonstrate the validity of the original argument indirectly. Demonstrations of validity can themselves be regarded as arguments. But whereas an argument need contain only a premise and conclusion, demonstrations of validity include a discourse, or some additional statements, that purport to account for the relationship between those propositions that define the basic argument. Premise-conclusion arguments claim validity only. Demonstrative arguments try to make this claim of validity intelligible by working explicitly to show why the claim must be valid.

The discourse in a demonstrative argument always includes laws or rules that appear as general statements and operate to connect the premise with the conclusion. What distinguishes these statements from the premise and conclusion is that they have a psychological as well as a logical function. The premise is logically necessary for the truth of the conclusion. Statements constituting the discourse share in this necessity; but they are also essential for psychological reasons. A person will frequently read or hear an argument and fail to see any relation between the premise and conclusion. The reason for this might be that there is no relation. But where the argument is valid, where the premise and conclusion are linked together objectively, failure to discern any connection can only be attributed to an incapacity or inability of the person to comprehend it. Either the person lacks sufficient knowledge to understand the argument or has failed to follow its logical steps. The purpose of the discourse is to remedy this situation by conveying the argument to a particular individual or group without distorting or destroying its logical force.

In general, most arguments fulfill both functions. That is, they are presented both as valid arguments and as arguments that can be perceived as valid. The discourse is usually integrated with the premise and cannot be easily separated out. Ordinarily this is quite proper. For, like the premise, the truth of the discourse is a necessary condition for the truth of the conclusion

and to this extent serves an identical function. If the
conclusion is accepted as true, the discourse must also
be accepted as true along with the premise. The
difference is that the discourse is needed for
psychological as well as logical reasons. Without it
validity could not be perceived.

One last point should be made about the general
features of arguments. Everyone recognizes that some
arguments are better than others, not simply for
psychological reasons or because they are valid, but
because they represent the truth. Valid arguments with
true premises are called sound. The conclusions are
therefore true because the premises are true. As with
valid arguments, sound arguments are not contingent on
being recognized as such. Their soundness is an objective
and, therefore, independent property. Arguments known
to be sound are demonstrative arguments, otherwise they
are what we have referred to as premise-conclusion
arguments. Sound demonstrative arguments can be perceived
as valid, but they must also have premises that are known
to be true.

THREE TYPES OF ARGUMENTS:
PROOFS, EXPLANATIONS, JUSTIFICATIONS

Arguments can be categorized according to the nature
of the inference they assume. Thus, we distinguish for
analytical purposes three types of arguments: proofs,
explanations, and justifications. Proofs answer the
question: Why is it conceptually assumed that p?; where
"p" is any formal proposition thought to be necessary
as a matter of logic. Explanations answer the question:
Why is it the case that p?; where "p" is any substantive
proposition the truth of which is presupposed.
Justifications answer the question: Why should it be
believed that p?; where "p" is any substantive proposition
the truth of which is at issue.

To specify the logic of these inferences with any
degree of clarity or precision can be an extremely
difficult task. Sometimes it seems that intuitive
understanding is the most we can hope for. But here
experience makes us suspicious. We learn to be leery
of our intuitions and not to leave them unexamined in
perpetuity. This is one reason philosophers continue
to take this problem so seriously. With proofs, they
have met with some success; with explanations, perhaps
less so; but with justifications, their efforts have been

almost fruitless. A brief examination of some of their
findings will make this obvious.

Proofs
       Proofs are both the strongest and weakest form of
rational argument. Their strength results from their
reliability. By proofs, we can be absolutely certain
whether the conclusions follow from the premises. These
arguments are referred to technically as "deductive."
In this kind of argument the conclusion is part of the
meaning of the premise. We say that the relationship
is one of "formal implication." The two help to define
each other. To accept the premise and reject the
conclusion would violate the principle of contradiction.
A proposition cannot be true and false. The
relationship between a premise and what it imples is like
that between a whole and its parts, the only difference
being that this relationship is purely conceptual.
       The weakness of deductive arguments is that they
have virtually no content. Their conclusions, about which
it is impossible to be mistaken, are utterly trivial,
"trivial" meaning, in a philosophical sense, "without
any real reference." Other types of arguments refer
directly to the world. They have what philosophers call
"existential import" and use language to talk about facts
and relations that have reality in their own right. But
proofs deal exclusively with the syntactic and semantic
properties of language. Language is used merely to
discuss language. Questions that cannot be formulated
in a metalanguage are ruled out of bounds. Conclusions
of proofs are analytic, their truth is solely a matter
of their logical form or the meaning of the words. We
call them formal propositions because they speak only
of the form of our thinking. They structure our ideas
without defining the substance of our thought. Put in
the technical terms of the logician, they reveal what
the logic of a language makes possible and they establish
the limits of what can be known a priori by those who
use that language.
       Proofs are sometimes thought of as arguments that
establish the truth of substantive propositions as well
as formal ones. In antiquity this view had considerable
merit. Truth was assumed to be objective and universal.
It represented the essence of things, as opposed to
attributes that were merely accidental. Truth may be
in the world, the ancients said, but it is not of
the world. Thus, it cannot be known through experience

or sense perception. Instead, a priori methods must be
used. This was the basis on which proofs became the
medium for gaining knowledge of ultimate reality. The
formal propositions of logic took on ontological
significance and proofs were regarded as equivalent to
the justification of nontrivial truth claims.
     Modern philosophy has altered these circumstances
radically. Truth is now seen as either subjective,
relative, or both. In consequence the distinction between
essence and attribute, between subject and predicate,
has become difficult if not impossible to maintain. The
reason for this has been the rise of philosophical
empiricism and the corresponding decline of philosophical
rationalism. Experience has become the measure of all
things. Generally we will concede that the only way to
acquire knowledge of existential import is through sense
perception. But this leaves a gap between formal logic
and ontology. If the formal propositions of logic are
known a priori and reality known only through experience,
then it would seem that these propositions are trivial
in the philosophical sense of being nonsubstantive. They
are merely figments of the imagination or creations of
the mind. Further, proofs of these propositions can only
be understood as a mode of argument quite distinct from
the justification of substantive knowledge claims.
     To speak of proofs in relation to nontrivial
propositions is strictly metaphorical. It means that
we have the evidence on our side, that these propositions
have been established empirically beyond all reasonable
doubt. Still, we cannot be absolutely certain. We
experience the consequences of things, not things as they
are in themselves. Our perceptions are always indirect
and our judgments always fallible. We are left with the
probabilities and vicissitudes of living and we can never
be guaranteed the reliable inferences found in formal
logic. Proofs offer us a paradigm of objectivity. They
have nothing to do with our feelings or opinions, but
focus instead on what is true independently of the
interests and needs of the knowing subject. But, alas,
this truth says nothing whatsoever about anything.

Explanations
     Few limits exist on what might be called an
explanation. Those who refuse or fail to recognize
different types of arguments will naturally use the terms
"proof," "explanation," and "justification" as more or
less synonymous. Moreover, to request an explanation

might be no more than to ask for additional information
or clarification of the meaning of ideas. Kaplan refers
to explanations of this latter sort as "semantic
explanations":

> A semantic explanation is a translation or
> paraphrase, a set of words having a meaning
> equivalent or similar to those being explained, but
> more easily or better understood. It is essential
> to semantic explanation that it serves as such only
> for someone or other. What is intelligible to one
> person may not be so to another; one person may not
> need an explanation at all, and for another the
> explanation given may be inadequate. If the person
> to whom the explanation is addressed doesn't "get
> it," the meaning just has not been explained. A
> semantic explanation, as Dewey once said of
> education, is the outcome of a transaction, a sale:
> the sale is not made unless the customer actually
> buys.[1]

However well we formulate a semantic explanation
it cannot possibly meet the conditions that define an
argument. It need not be expressed as a set of related
propositions, for one thing; and for another, it will
not have a conclusion that is thought to follow
necessarily from a premise. Another difference is that
the concepts of validity and soundness will have no
bearing on the evaluation of the explanation. Excepting,
perhaps, for service as the discourse in demonstrations
of validity, explanations of this sort display few of
the features identified as essential to arguments.
    When conceived as a special type of argument,
explanations represent more than mere explications of
meaning. Although they may be offered up to a consumer
for acceptance, they are not relative to the consumer
in the same manner as semantic explanations. An
explanation may account for the truth even though no one
believes it. The difference between a semantic
explanation and one conceived as a special type of
argument is like the difference between a statement's
being clear and its being true. In order to be clear
there must be someone for whom it is clear. But while

---

1.   Abraham Kaplan, The Conduct of Inquiry (San Francisco:
     Chandler, 1964) pp. 327-28.

it might be correct to say that in order for it to be
true for someone, someone must believe it, or have
evidence for it, or something of that kind, we could not
regard the truth of the statement as such in any way
contingent on anyone's accepting it as true.[2] In this
respect explanations conceived as a special type of
argument are like any other type of argument—whether
they are valid is not a question of anyone's perception.

    In addition to possessing the characteristics common
to arguments generally, explanations, when thought of
in this second sense, are concerned with more than ideas
and their formal implications. They assume the existence
of an independent and objective reality and purport to
account for events, occurrences, or happenings that take
place within the context of our dealings with that world.
Thus, unlike proofs, they have existential import and
generate conclusions that have ontological significance.
From the perspective of a thoroughgoing empiricism, the
events, occurrences, or happenings to be explained exist
exclusively within the limits of space and time. That
is to say, they may occur anywhere so long as they occur
somewhere, and may happen anytime so long as they happen
sometime. Given this principle, explanations are always
relative, not because their validity is contingent on
their being accepted, but because, according to the
Empiricist, they correspond to events located within an
expanse that has a past, a present, and a future.

    If the validity of an explanation was contingent
on its being accepted, then, by definition, it would be
subjective. To deny this is to say that validity
guarantees objectivity. The Empiricist does not
necessarily reject this principle. What the Empiricist
contends is that insofar as their conclusions are
contingent on their premises, all valid arguments are
relative. But more significantly for valid explanations,
the premises are themselves contingent and continually
susceptible to change. The world we experience is
constantly being transformed. As circumstances are
altered, so too must explanations be altered. This
dimension distinguishes explanations from proofs. Proofs
assume conditions that are universal. In a logical world
where arguments are purely conceptual this presents no
problems, generates no conflicts, and results in no
mistakes. But when the world is physical, biological,

---

2. Ibid., p. 328.

and social, and where arguments are substantive, any such assumption is unwarranted.

Proofs focus on the logical system that we use for thinking and are judged on the basis of conceptual clarity and internal consistency. Explanations put this system to work. They employ the rules of syntax and meaning in a manner designed to provide understanding of a world that includes more than a rational mind. The criterion for an explanation's being valid is correspondence with this objective reality. The distinction in logic between formal and material implication is best interpreted as a distinction between proofs and explanations. Proofs deal exclusively with relationships between ideas; explanations deal with relationships between facts. In the latter case, validity cannot be established solely on the basis of conceptual clarity and internal consistency. Besides having to be conceivable, relationships between premises and conclusions must coincide with some actual state of affairs.

Given this distinction solipsism is an absurd doctrine. Objective reality is not simply the creation of consciousness. Explanations are relative, in the sense of being contingent, because they are valid within the limits of a specifiable context, not because they are subjective. When constructing an explanation ..e are more like an executive formulating policy, or even like a secretary taking dictation, than like an artist creating a scene on a canvas. Our efforts are to be judged not in terms of our preferences, but in experiential terms; in other words, on the basis of whether they link up with the world of our practical experience, and ultimately, we must say, with the world that is there.[3]

Justifications

Justifications are like proofs and explanations in that their validity is not a matter of opinion. In order to be sound they must be clear--they must communicate.

---

3. The phrase, "the world that is there," is taken from the work of G. H. Mead. See Mead, The Philosophy of the Act, ed. Charles W. Morris (Chicago: Univ. of Chicago Press, 1938), especially pp. 96, 257, 260-61. For an interpretation by a former student of Mead's see David L. Miller, George Herbert Mead--Self, Language, and the World (Austin: Univ. of Texas Press, 1973), especially chap. 5, pp. 88-102.

But whether or not they are accepted as valid is beside
the point.   Why, then, classify justifications as a
special type of argument?   The answer, as stated earlier,
is that they represent a unique kind of inference.
Whereas explanations account for the truth, justifications
establish the truth; not in the formal sense of a proof,
but in the substantive or material sense that is assumed
by explanations.
     What was said about explanations in this regard also
applies to justifications.   They are concerned with more
than relationships between ideas.   They assume the
existence of an independent and objective "world that
is there" and purport to depict the quantitative and
qualitative properties that constitute reality within
the context of our dealings with that world.   Thus, they
have existential import and generate conclusions having
ontological significance.   That justifications employ
a system of syntax and meaning is undeniable.   But as
substantive arguments their validity is a matter of
agreement with external facts and relations and is not
simply a function of their conceptual clarity and internal
consistency.
     An Empiricist would insist that since substantive
knowledge can only be gained through experience, that
is, through sense perception, justifications are
necessarily relative; not just because their conclusions
are contingent on their premises, but more profoundly
because these contingencies are similarly susceptible
to change.   As with explanations, this does not mean that
the validity of justifications is contingent on their
being accepted or (saying the same thing) that
justifications are unavoidably subjective.   More modestly,
it means that their validity is relative to conditions
that are themselves contingent and that, being something
less than universal, they cannot qualify as eternal
verities.
     Here too it would seem that solipsism is an absurd
doctrine.   For it considers the idea of agreement with
external facts and relations to be a myth, or worse yet,
as totally unintelligible.   In its most extreme form
solipsism concedes only that justifications represent
a certain type of argument.   That is to say, a
justification is a set of two or more propositions one
of which is inferred from the other in a manner that
purportedly establishes its truth.   So long as the
conclusion rests on at least one identifiable premise,

it has been justified in the only sense in which the term
"justified" can be rationally understood. To ask if the
argument were valid or sound, or if it had existential
import, as if these were questions over and above asking
if it were a certain type of argument would be seen as
hopelessly confused.

A second, less extreme form of solipsism acknowledges
that there is a distinction between a set of propositions
that constitutes an argument and a set of propositions
that constitutes a good argument. A good argument is
one that is accepted by those to whom it is addressed.
Thus, we can say on the basis of a clear and definite
standard that some justifications are better than others;
specifically, those that find an approving audience.
But notice, it would still be foolish to ask if a
justification were valid or sound, or if it had
existential import in addition to being accepted by those
to whom it was addressed. Solipsism may be less extreme
in this case; but here, as before, reality is conceived
as subjective, the only difference being that impressions
are those of the group rather than those of the
individual. Group solipsism which regards truth as
intersubjective differs only in degree from the view that
truth is subjectively defined, the view of individual
solipsism. Truth remains a matter of opinion on both
accounts.

Solipsism is especially vexing for Empiricists.
Believing that all substantive knowledge is based on
experience, they are committed to what Charles Peirce
called "fallibilism," or the view that absolute certainty
is unattainable in principle when applied to nontrivial
truth claims. As a consequence the distinction between
appearance and reality becomes difficult to draw. The
question is, can Empiricists admit this without denying
the distinction altogether? Most Empiricists believe
they can. They argue that while the individual begins
with crude and superficial sense perception, or what might
alternatively be described as first impressions, critical
examination of these perceptions, that is, rigorous and
disciplined inquiry, will finally unearth what is real.
We can discover objective truth through study that is
thoughtful and experimentally, or at least empirically,
based.

Thus, on this analysis, appearance is equated with
experience that is raw, unconsidered, and untested, while
reality is identified with experience that has been

intelligently conceived, analyzed, and appraised. Peirce
said of experience: "[it] . . . may be set down as one
of the most mendacious witnesses that ever was questioned.
But it is the only witness there is; and all we can do
is to put it in the sweat-box and torture the truth out
of it, with such judgment as we can command."[4] Though
the process provides no basis for certainty, what results
is far from mere appearance. Truth is expressed as
reasoned judgments made within a context of physical and
social activity. Correspondingly, these judgments serve
as objective and evolutionary descriptions of reality.
While arguments that support them are circumstantial and
may turn out to be invalid or misleading, they are not
on that account irrational or subjective.

      This means, first, that judgments, by their very
definition, always leave room for error. When expressed
as propositions they can never be known with absolute
certainty and logically might be false. To be certain
in a logical sense, or to know something for sure, is
to deny the judgmental function. We can be certain in
the psychological sense of having conviction or faith.
But this, obviously, is not the same as demonstrating
that the contrary is inconceivable, as would be required
by a strict logic. However, of equal importance, neither
are judgments mere guesses. Guesses are hunches; we might
call them "subjective opinions," for they lack an
intelligible foundation. Judgments, on the other hand,
are informed by evidence, reasons, and standards. Thomas
Green tells us:

      They are never subjective in the sense of having
      sole reference to the feelings, preferences, or
      subjective states of the speaker. They are never
      subjective in the sense that statements about one's
      feelings, preferences, and dispositions are
      subjective. They are always objective in the sense
      that they rest upon reasons, grounds, rules, or
      principles. . . . The fact that reasonable men may
      differ in their judgment does not imply that they
      are merely expressing some personal preference or

---

4. C. S. Peirce, Collected Papers of Charles Sanders
    Peirce, Vol. 1, ed. Charles Hartshorne and Paul Weiss
    (Cambridge: Harvard Univ. Press, 1965), p. 318
    (1.580).

a mere groundless opinion. . . . Nor does it imply
that in such matters any man's opinion is as good
as another's. Clearly, there is a difference between
discerning judgments and mere flippant or casual
opinions; and that difference is roughly the same
as the contrast between making a judgment and
offering a mere guess or hunch.[5]

Good judgment is an expression of practical wisdom
that allows us to estimate, rank, predict, or adjudicate
with a maximum degree of accuracy in circumstances where
certain knowledge is unattainable or inaccessible. As
Green puts it: "To exercise good judgment is to get
optimum results under less than optimum conditions or
on grounds which are less than decisive."[6] To
characterize a judgment as subjective is to claim that
it is biased, distorted, shortsighted, or blind to
relevant information, but not literally that it is
whimsical or capricious. A subjective judgment is simply
out of step with reality and cannot be defended or
justified as having high probability. Yet, it remains
a statement of probability and can be understood and
appraised within the logic of experience.

On this analysis, which is inherent in empiricism,
the truth of substantive propositions can never be
guaranteed even by the most scrupulously formulated
justifications. The most we can hope for is to establish
them as true--as we might say in a courtroom--"beyond
all reasonable doubt." To guarantee their truth implies
infallibility. To establish their truth demands only
that they be worthy of belief by an intelligent observer.
Insofar as truth is objective it is not contingent on
being known and, thus, not contingent on evidence or
arguments adduced in its behalf. Substantive propositions
worthy of belief by an intelligent observer are
propositions known on the basis of experience and reason,
even though this might entail something less than absolute
certainty. Where truth has been established, claims to
know have been adequately supported but never assured.
From a logical point of view, truth does not imply
justification, nor does justification imply truth.

---

5. Thomas F. Green, The Activities of Teaching (New
   York: McGraw-Hill, 1971), p. 178.
6. Ibid., p. 177.

This point has special significance when applied
to questions of value. Showing that normative
propositions (that is, propositions as to the value or
worth of things) are justified does not necessitate
showing with absolute certainty that they are true. To
this extent they are like factual propositions. Whether
they are justified depends on whether they are reasonable
to believe. It is enough to demonstrate that intelligence
demands their acceptance and, correspondingly, that to
live by their negation would be foolish.

C H A .P T E R   3

CREATING AND USING STANDARDS

This chapter has three objectives: first, on the assumption that there is an important distinction between descriptive and prescriptive propositions, to suggest a technique for distinguishing them, even in bewildering cases where distinctions are not easily come by; second, on the assumption that there is a difference between creating a standard (a criterion) and using it, to suggest means for identifying each respective endeavor; and third, on the assumption that the creation of a standard is not obviously dependent on the existence of particular facts, to begin to say something in support of the view, often referred to as naturalism or descriptivism, that judgments of value have an objective relation to judgments of fact.

DESCRIPTIVE AND PRESCRIPTIVE PROPOSITIONS

While most people are not conscious of a distinction between descriptive and prescriptive propositions, the difference seems obvious once it is pointed out. Descriptive propositions tell us what in fact is the case. Prescriptive propositions tell us what should or ought to be the case.

Philosophers have said of descriptive propositions that they possess cognitive content, meaning simply that their truth is not a question of subjective opinion. My saying, for example, that positive reinforcement is more effective than negative reinforcement in establishing learned patterns of behavior is a fact, if true, independent of my preferences, or so it would seem. My saying it is a fact does not make it a fact. Descriptions

need to be verified through observation and testing in
order to establish the implicit judgments as sound, at
least to the extent they are empirical. By definition,
propositions we classify as descriptions do not create
the facts they describe. They necessarily assume the
prior presence of appropriate existential referents.
On the other hand, prescriptive propositions tell us what
ought to be the case, regardless of what is the case.
That children should understand the heritage of their
race might provide us with an example of this.

BEWILDERING CASES
     So far all this is old hat. Philosophers have long
said that descriptions do not entail prescriptions, and
vice versa. Most people will agree once they are provided
with the classic rationale. But wait! Something needs
to be said about those not infrequent cases we find
bewildering, cases where it is hard to tell whether
propositions are descriptive or prescriptive. The
distinction itself is unassailable, so propositions must
be one or the other and we need to know because where
classification is beyond our ken, it is impossible to
comprehend fully or appraise rationally what is said.
But perhaps most importantly of all, bewildering cases
make it impossible to understand precisely the relation
between facts and values. Comprehension of this relation
is founded on the clear-cut recognition of propositions
as being of one sort or the other. For this reason it
is important to possess some method or technique that
will allow us to classify them, in virtually every
significant case, as either descriptive or prescriptive.
     We can begin with four examples of what might be
regarded as bewildering cases:

1.   Intelligence is determined by speed of calculation.
2.   Teaching is an activity that excludes indoctrination.
3.   An emotionally stable child should be offered
     intrinsic rather than extrinsic incentives.
4.   A child should never be overly motivated by self or
     others.

     The first two examples are written in the form of
"is" statements, that is, descriptive propositions. If
they state facts, however, it is not obvious. The latter

two examples are written in the form of "ought" statements, that is, prescriptive propositions. Here we must say that if they do not state facts, it is not obvious. Surely these examples demonstrate that the distinction between descriptive and prescriptive propositions is not simply a matter of vocabulary. "Is" often means "ought" and vice versa. Having been told that intelligence is determined by speed of calculation, some of us would register the remark as normative. We require some evidence to the contrary if we are told to view it otherwise, for the assertion appears to be "simply" a value preference. To say that speed of calculation is more important than, say, individual initiative, accuracy, or breadth of knowledge is not to describe, but to say how intelligence ought to be conceived, or so it would seem. It appears to reflect a condition that we are asked to prize. The truth of the proposition is contingent on a selected standard of excellence. If the standard were to change, so would our description of what we see. It would seem that a description of this circumstance is better seen as a judgment of value than a judgment of fact. The description of behavior as "intelligent" might be more profoundly understood as a judgment of the worth of that behavior.

On the other hand, if we are told that we should provide intrinsic incentives to an emotionally stable child, we are in all likelihood being given information that has precious little to do with a judgment of what is morally right. Assertions of this kind normally imply predictions of what will happen under certain specifiable conditions. We are not usually fooled by the mere appearance of words like "is" and "should" into thinking of propositions as descriptive or normative. The distinction here is not merely a vocabulary one. Anyone who says so runs the risk of regarding factual judgments as judgments of value and value judgments as judgments of fact. Actually, we classify propositions according to their function, not their grammatical form. And it is here where problems in their analysis first arise.

Philosophers have frequently bemoaned the difficulties of devising a descriptive language free from subjective bias and/or moral appraisal. Certainly there are times when the generation of value-free descriptions would seem to require exceptional ingenuity. But some will conclude on purely logical grounds that the task, like that of producing a perpetual motion machine, is impossible. To say, for example, that someone is strong or tall, like saying that something is desirable, commits one to the standards inherent in the conceptions of strong and tall. And those standards, so the argument goes, cannot themselves be established as facts, even in principle.

We might conclude from this, as some have, that all language is prescriptive, or, more simply, that there is no distinction worth keeping between descriptive and prescriptive propositions. Either conclusion, however, would be premature. A distinction so deeply ingrained in our thinking is not likely to occur without purpose. But even if we assume that there is such a purpose and, furthermore, admit to its importance, two nagging questions remain. First: What is this purpose, exactly? Second: How is the distinction to be understood if not merely as a vocabulary distinction? We can deal with the first of these questions in a rather cavalier manner, since the second question is more troublesome and ultimately determines the answer to the first.

Descriptions perform an important linguistic function: they report the facts. In the sense in which "function" means "purpose," the purpose of descriptive propositions is synonymous with this function. Likewise for prescriptions. They function linguistically to direct what we do. Here too we can say that this function constitutes their purpose. As two distinct modes of communication, descriptive and prescriptive propositions have a practical payoff, and this payoff both defines and justifies their linguistic separation. This claim follows John Dewey's distinction between the verb and the noun forms of "to value." When used as a verb "to value" means "to appraise or estimate the worth of something." In this sense, values are primarily instrumental. The intellectual aspects of things valued are uppermost. Concern is primarily with the relational attributes of existential facts. When used as a noun "to value" means "to prize, to hold precious or dear." Thus, what is valued elicits strong emotional attachment and personal identification. In the first instance, values result from a process of evaluation and represent descriptive propositions, in other words, factual judgments. In the latter instance, values result from a process of valuation and represent prescriptive propositions, that is, value judgments.[1]

If it is granted that descriptive and prescriptive propositions represent two distinct modes of communication, it is still an open question whether justifiable prescriptions are objectively related to particular facts. But that neither is reducible to the other would appear to be quite beyond dispute.

BRUTE FACTS AND INSTITUTIONAL FACTS

But now the question is: How are we to understand the distinction between these two kinds of propositions? That there is a distinction is one thing; how it is to be logically conceived is quite another. If we should not be bullied into denying the reality of this distinction by our failure to state it in precise intellectual terms, neither should we deceive ourselves into thinking that we understand it simply because we know that it exists.

We can get some help here. John R. Searle and before him G. E. M. Anscombe proposed to differentiate between two kinds of facts, "brute facts" and "institutional facts."[2] Brute facts were understood as sheer movements or bare ontological states that have a minimum of psychological and social significance. To say, for example, that a person is six feet tall or has brown hair is to assert what would normally be classified as brute facts. Institutional facts were thought of as brute facts that have taken on some degree of psychological and social prominence. To say someone is cultured or highly educated, for example, is to claim the existence of what can only be regarded as institutional facts. Institutional facts presuppose social conventions, or what might better be termed "values." They assume the operation of norms. Take away social conventions and

1. See John Dewey, Theory of Valuation, International Encyclopedia of the Unified Sciences (Chicago: Univ. of Chicago Press, 1939).
2. G. E. M. Anscombe, "On Brute Facts," Analysis, 18 (1958), 69-72. John R. Searle, "Deriving 'Ought' from 'Is,'" Speech Acts (New York: Cambridge Univ. Press, 1969).

being cultured or highly educated involves little more
than making physical gestures and/or verbal utterances.
Like winning a point in tennis, they owe their existence
to the rules of the game.

In short, without social conventions facts are always
brute. But being cultured or highly educated does involve
more than making physical gestures and/or verbal
utterances. When reduced to brute facts institutional
facts lose their intended and essential meaning. We
cannot say that being cultured or highly educated means
only to make physical gestures and/or verbal utterances,
for they imply a sense of understanding and appreciation
that cannot be captured solely through material
description. Recognizing that institutional facts are
rightly regarded as facts, and that we cannot preserve
their meaning by reducing them to facts that are brute,
we can only suppose that in this and other examples there
are two kinds of facts, and not just one.

In bewildering cases where we cannot easily
categorize a proposition as descriptive or prescriptive
the reason is usually that, while obviously not denoting
a simple brute fact, it is not obviously a prescription
either. In such cases the proposition is usually based
on the assumption of an institutional fact. When it is
we can regard it correctly as descriptive. But now the
problem becomes: How can we determine if a proposition
is based on the assumption of an institutional fact?
By following this principle: <u>If all parties to the
discourse in which the proposition is issued accept the
institution assumed in the proposition, then the
proposition is descriptive; otherwise the proposition
is prescriptive.</u> When the institution is not unanimously
accepted, work needs to be done to establish, or, perhaps,
alter operational norms.

The rationale underlying this principle is as
follows: propositions that assume institutional facts
are not descriptive by virtue of their referents alone.
Their classification as descriptive is as much a matter
of common agreement as it is a matter of what, perchance,
they denote. Admittedly, the use of common agreement
as a criterion for classifying propositions makes the
descriptive label relative to existing social relations.
It would be a mistake, however, to conclude that this
makes the process of classification subjective or
arbitrary, because first, common agreement is the essence

of any institution. As such it need not always be conscious; we need not always be aware of our agreement. It might even be expressed in a form that transcends the individual altogether and thereby acquires a life of its own. Thus, there may be common agreement as to a particular value or mode of behavior even though no one any longer prizes this thing or acts this way. Under such circumstances the value or mode of behavior symbolizes an ideal of the society or culture as a whole, defining truth and goodness and retaining the sanctions of tradition. Common agreement is a necessary condition for the emergence of institutional facts. Once having lost this ideal status they can have no ontological standing.

Second, to hold that for propositions assuming institutional facts the descriptive label is relative to existing social relations is equivalent to the view that these propositions remain descriptive only so long as they are intended in reference to that particular objective context. It is not to say that as descriptions they are true or accurate, and most certainly it is not to say that their descriptive classification is subjective or arbitrary.

So now we have a technique for categorizing bewildering cases as descriptive or prescriptive propositions. Look to see if the institution assumed by the proposition is accepted, in the sense specified above, by all parties to the discourse. If so, then the proposition is descriptive. Moreover, it is true if the standards it assumes are met by the situation to which it applies. If not, then it is false. In either case, however, the proposition is descriptive. If the institution assumed by the proposition is not accepted, then the assertion is prescriptive. Parties having an interest in the discourse must then work for agreement on existing or alternative operational norms.

REGULATIVE RULES AND CONSTITUTIVE RULES

Still another question needs answering, however: Once we have categorized a proposition as descriptive of an institutional fact or as prescriptive, how can we analyze the difference? We might rest content by saying that in the former case standards are being used, while in the latter standards are being created, usually with an accompanying effort to establish them as justified.[3] But how can we tell when standards are being used and when they are being created? To answer this question we need to employ the now common philosophical notions of regulative and constitutive rules.

Regulative rules presuppose antecedently existing forms of activity. That is, regulative rules regulate activity the existence of which is assumed to be independent of regulative rules. For example, the rules of etiquette are customarily understood to regulate the activity of eating. But one can eat without observing these rules. Constitutive rules do more than regulate activity, they create or define it. Hence, the existence of the activity is assumed to depend logically on the operation of these rules. For instance, in baseball the rule, "Three strikes and you're out," does more than regulate the activity of playing baseball. It helps to define the game. Failure to observe the rule means that one is not playing baseball. Not simply that one is not playing it properly or well, but rather that one is not playing baseball at all; for baseball cannot be played apart from the operation of this rule.

An extremely important feature of both kinds of rules needs to be made more explicit. What makes a rule regulative or constitutive is determined by how it is regarded. The rules of etiquette could be seen as so fundamental that they defined whether someone was eating, as opposed to, say, merely passing food through their body. Likewise, the rule for striking out might not be seen as essential to baseball if, let us suppose, it determined only the batting stance of the player hitting the ball. In the first case, the rules of etiquette would be constitutive; and in the second, the rule for striking out would be regulative. The fact they are not so regarded by the majority of influential rulemakers means that the rules of etiquette are not constitutive and the rule for striking out is not just regulative. But that this is a function of how they are regarded is an observation too important to ignore.

---

3. The distinction between creating and using standards is intended in the same sense as Dewey's distinction between prizing and appraising, or, more precisely, between the process of valuation and the process of evaluation.

Only, how do these two conceptions of rules enable us to tell when standards are being used and when they are being created? We must remember first that whether being used or created, standards are expressed as propositions. Like all propositions their meanings are based on the roles they play in human communication. Now a role is structured by rules. As rules are divided into kinds according to their differentiating functions, so too the kinds of propositions designating standards result from the kinds of rules that give them meaning. Thus, knowing that the meaning of a proposition is governed by a certain kind of rule enables one to know what kind of proposition it represents.

If, in a particular situation, the rules that structure the role of a proposition are regulative rules, existing standards are being used, and the proposition is properly classified as descriptive of an institutional fact.

This point of view has the following rationale: The operation of regulative rules presupposes the existence of prior activity, activity logically independent of these rules. The proposition cannot be about whether a certain sort of activity is going on, but only about whether it is being conducted properly or well. The concern cannot be about what is or is not meaningful, but only about what is or is not true.

By way of illustration, the proposition that someone is intelligent is a descriptive proposition if the rules that give it meaning are regarded as regulative. What defines intelligence in this case is simply not at issue, it is assumed. The problem is to apply the standards to a particular individual to see if, as a matter of fact, that person is intelligent. The institution of intelligence goes unchallenged here. We are not to conceptualize or define the matter, but only to describe an actually existing state of affairs.

On the other hand, if, in a particular situation, the rules that structure the role of a proposition are constitutive, then standards are being created or set up, and the proposition is properly classified as prescriptive. Since the activity is not assumed to exist independently of the operation of these rules, the use of standards, if a function at all, is not the primary function of the proposition. The proposition in this case is like an axiom or postulate that is not intended to correspond with an antecedently existing reality.

As prescriptive it is designed to give significance to what heretofore has been of little interest or has had no ontological standing at all.

Now we have two techniques. One allows us, at least in principle, to categorize propositions, even those we find bewildering, as descriptive or prescriptive. The other allows us to decide unequivocally, if only in principle, whether a proposition is designed to use or create standards. If it is designed to use standards, but not to create them, then the proposition is descriptive of institutional facts and can be verified, one is tempted to say, empirically, as true or false, at least in principle. Otherwise it is prescriptive.

JUSTIFICATIONS AND PROOFS

But now a new question appears. Is there any sense in which prescriptions can be spoken of as justified? More to the point: How do true descriptive propositions bear on the justification of prescriptions, if at all? How descriptive propositions bear on prescriptions is a question better put in terms of judgments. How do judgments of fact bear on judgments of value, if at all? Some philosophers have objected to this reduction. They have insisted that prescriptive propositions are straightforward logical implications from descriptive propositions and that, therefore, prescriptions are not judgments. Thus, the two questions are not the same. In his essay on deriving "ought" from "is" Searle argues that what ought to be can at least sometimes be implied formally, as a matter of logical necessity, from a description of the facts. That one man ought to give another a certain sum of money, for example depends upon whether the first man promised to do so. If, as a matter of fact, he did so promise, then by implication he ought to pay up. From the fact that x did y, so the argument goes, we can infer a priori that x ought to do p. Simple! But not really.

Based on what has already been said it should be clear that what Searle calls a prescription is not really a prescription at all. If there is a prescription to be found in his argument, it is located in the set of propositions serving as his premises; more particularly, his assertion that x did y, that someone made a promise. The claim that someone who made a promise ought to pay up presupposes that a standard has been used and a fact

determined that a promise was actually made. The
determination of the fact, the factual judgment, is
rightly taken as descriptive. When we are using
standards, as opposed to creating and/or giving them
support, what appears as a prescription, as a normative
conclusion, is really a proposition we can know to be
true as a matter of logic. We can know it as an
implication from what we know to be factually true.

About Searle's example we can say, in effect, that
given the institution of promising and the justified
factual judgment that our man made a promise, he ought
to pay up, "as a matter of fact." But we must still
insist that prescriptions represent judgments. Indeed,
to say so is analytic. If it were true that the
conclusion in Searle's example was prescriptive, then
the question of the relation between descriptive and
prescriptive propositions could not be reduced to the
question of the relation between factual judgments and
value judgments. But it is not, so there is no apparent
reason to think that the reduction is not legitimate.

The use of standards in arguments is not unique to
justifications. It is a feature common to all arguments.
Justifying the use of a standard, that is, arguing that
a standard is being employed correctly, represents a
factual judgment, not a value judgment. Searle's example
deriving "ought" from "is" involves a rather complex use
of a standard. Included is a claim about the meaning
of the standard and an attempt to show that it is being
employed properly. Arguments to be adduced in support
of what is said would include a proof and a justification
of a judgment of fact.

While thinking he had solved the "is/ought problem,"
Searle showed instead that the distinction between "is"
and "ought" is not merely a vocabulary distinction. That
"Jones ought to pay Smith five dollars," like "A
quarterback should always pass on third and five," is
a case where a standard is being used. The standard can
be inferred from other propositions symbolizing
definitions, observations, and judgments of fact. The
conditions under which a person can correctly be said
to have made a promise are usually regarded, quite
properly, as factual. When they are, the contention that
a promise made ought to be kept is analytic.

Undoubtedly there are times when it is incumbent
to challenge existing standards, such as those that define
promise-making, for example. It would surely be perverse,

however, to act as if it were always reasonable to reject
prevailing institutions. Antony Flew and others have
pointed out an important distinction between those who
use existing linguistic conventions to issue detached
reports on the meaning of normative words and those who
use them as engaged participants.[4] The distinction
is crucial, for it separates those like Searle, who want
simply to describe and/or understand reality as it is,
from those who want to evaluate or morally appraise that
reality. Only from this latter perspective do we find
that commitment to incapsulated values that alone warrants
the classification of propositions as prescriptive.

FACTS AND VALUES
     At last we can see the fundamental issue and can
tackle it head-on. When we create and/or express a
commitment to standards are we involved in a rational
activity that is based on factual observations, or does
this activity represent a more or less arbitrary
expression of personal taste? Until recently the thrust
of twentieth-century value theory has suggested the
latter. Not only members of the now historic Vienna
Circle and such early Emotivists as A. J. Ayer and C. L.
Stevenson, but even more recently R. M. Hare and A. G. N.
Flew, have taken a position on this matter not unlike
the view of most contemporary Phenomenalists and
Existentialists. All have argued, quite persuasively,
that standards of value are matters of choice dependent
solely on feeling and sentiment. And unlike John Dewey,
or even David Hume (1711-1776), they have insisted that
feeling and sentiment are manifestations of personal
subjectivity. The conclusion is that no relationships
can be rationally justified between what is valued and
the way things are. The idea of objective standards of
value empirically based has been discarded by these
writers as a superstitious obsession.
     This analysis has been heard from before in the
history of philosophy, but rarely has it been argued with
such cogency. All the same, philosophers are now

----

4.   A. G. N. Flew, "On Not Deriving 'Ought' from 'Is,'"
     The Is-Ought Question, ed. W. D. Hudson (New York:
     Macmillan, 1969), pp. 135-43.

beginning to look at it with some skepticism. Not that
they are reverting to the questionable metaphysics that
precipitated the Subjectivists' reaction, but, more
simply, they are putting greater stock in intelligence
and human inquiry. While admitting that a person can
always deny on logical grounds that a particular fact
must be valued, they do not think it follows that anything
whatsoever can be rationally valued. G. J. Warnock has
argued, in the spirit of John Dewey, that while there
are, perhaps, no logical limits to what a person could
be said to want, or to things that everyone might be said
to want, there are limits to what a person could be said
"understandably" to want.[5]

      To specify what this means and to show its
significance and credibility as a general theory of value
remains the objective for the chapters that follow.
Toward this end we will examine the classical metaphysical
view of values, or the view that will sometimes be called
formalism. We will also examine the Subjectivist school,
or the view that will sometimes be called nominalism.
Nominalists maintain that arguments as to the value or
worth of things can be distinguished only by their logical
properties. Yet this, we will say, is mistaken. We will
say further that Formalists seem to be wrong in their
metaphysics, but right in their placing emphasis on the
content of disputes about values. As we will see,
normative arguments deal ultimately with questions of
human welfare. And justifiable standards contribute
directly or indirectly to human betterment. Therein are
justifiable judgments of value distinguishable from
justifiable judgments of fact. Therein are moral
arguments distinguishable from those that are morally
neutral.

      If there is little agreement and much debate over
what is good and how people should live, the cause stems
not from logical oddities that characterize normative
arguments, but rather from the recalcitrance of human
nature. Why should we not believe that understanding
human beings makes it easier to resolve questions of value
and moral propriety? Charles Kingsley (1819-1875) once
remarked, "Be good, sweet maid, and let who will be

---

5. G. J. Warnock, Contemporary Moral Philosophy (New
   York: Macmillan, 1967), p. 66.

clever." But in our time it is painfully obvious that
virtue requires knowledge, and, without genuine
understanding, what passes for goodness is nothing but
arrogance and self-righteous conceit.

CHAPTER 4

INTUITIONISM AS A THEORY OF VALUE: A CONCESSION TO FORMALISM

From the time of the Greeks, and for the better part of the history of western culture, thinking about values has been dominated by formalism. Within the classical tradition values are conceived as objective, nonnatural properties. Their objectivity is simply assumed. Their status as nonnatural properties is inferred a priori, as a matter of logic, from this postulation of objectivity.

To begin with, objectivity is thought to imply universality. That is to say, nothing can be objective without also being universal. And since, by definition, everything in nature is subject to change, since nothing in nature is universal, values being objective are necessarily nonnatural properties. More precisely, values may be _in_ the world, in the sense we might speak of ghosts or a divine force as being "in the world," but they cannot be _of_ the world in the same manner as things physical lest they lose their objectivity.

If values are a force in the world, it is nonetheless true that they are not the result of experience and can never be detected by empirical means. They can only be known by means that transcend experience, some form of direct perception not mediated by sensations or physical signs. If knowledge gained through experience is limited to the kingdom of nature, we must rely for our knowledge of values on pure reason, intuition, meditation, contemplation, or some other type of a priori method.

With the rise of empiricism and science this view was seriously undermined. Any idea not rooted in experience was given little credibility. Within intellectual circles the tendency was to define values in terms of such natural properties as happiness, pleasure, power, or knowledge--properties that could be understood and verified by ordinary people in ordinary ways. But alas, this program of reconstruction turned out to have problems of its own and by the beginning of the twentieth century many philosophers, including some who were to be counted among the most rigorous Empiricists, were ready to reconsider formalism as a viable theory of value. Perhaps, the best example of this phenomenon was the British philosopher G. E. Moore.

Moore, a philosopher of exceptional ability and considerable influence, was by no means at his best when writing on the topic of values. Yet, despite this, Principia Ethica, first published in 1903, is a good deal more interesting than the work of most Intuitionists and is unquestionably far more important.[1] He says in the opening pages that his sole business is with "that object or idea" which the word "good" "is generally used to stand for."[2] Strangely enough, he goes out of his way in the preface to "beg it may be noticed that, I am not an 'Intuitionist,' in the ordinary sense of the term."[3] Whereas, generally, Intuitionists believe that values, and especially moral values, can always be known through intuition, Moore maintains that intuition can be used only in relation to a very small class of basic values. This difference undoubtedly weighs in Moore's favor. But the fact remains that he allows for truths that are self-evident, truths that can be known directly, without proof, evidence, or argument, and to this extent he could hardly object to being classified as an Intuitionist, since this is exactly what the term is meant to imply.

Moore believed that what is good, morally or otherwise, can be described as an objective property or quality. This means that values, whether moral or nonmoral, designate facts. But how, we might ask, can they be distinguished from facts that are not values, assuming, of course, that not all facts are values? Moore

---

1. This view, with slight modifications, represents the judgment of G. J. Warnock. See Contemporary Moral Philosophy (New York: Macmillan, 1967), p. 4.
2. George Edward Moore, Principia Ethica (Cambridge, England: Cambridge Univ. Press, 1968), p. 6.
3. Ibid., p. x.

answered this question indirectly, that is, he gave a
negative definition, by stating what values are not.
Values are not, he said, reducible to other facts. Values
cannot be defined in terms of objective properties or
qualities that are not themselves values. To equate
values with happiness, pleasure, power, or knowledge,
for example, is to identify them with what as a matter
of fact they are not. Following Bishop Joseph Butler
(1692-1752), Moore said, "Everything is what it is, and
not another thing." Values cannot be identified except
with themselves, nor expressed in anything but their own
terms because, according to Moore, they are unique.

If values could be defined in terms of facts that
were not themselves values, or values exclusively, it
would be true by definition, or analytic, to say that
these facts had value. Put somewhat more technically,
if having value could be equated with p, and "p" were
any property that encompassed more than having value,
then it would be a simple point of logic to say that p
has value and, correspondingly, a formal contradiction
to deny that p has value. But this, as Moore was quick
to point out, is never the case. Given any clear
conception of value, it always remains an open question
to ask whether p has value, the reason being that the
question is substantive and can never be answered purely
by dialectical means.

Moore made a second claim about values, or at least
about basic values, which, while still negative, would,
like the first, have enormous significance if it were
true. He declared, not only is it impossible to reduce
values to nonvalue properties, but neither can values
be rightly regarded as properties of nature. To do either
or both of these things is to commit what Moore called,
"the naturalistic fallacy." He came to the second part
of this conclusion indirectly, by eliminating all other
possibilities. If, as he said, we cannot detect the
presence or absence of values empirically, it would be
preposterous to say that we can experience them in
anything like the standard sense, or literally observe
them as we might, for example, literally observe physical
objects. If values were natural properties, they could,
at least in principle, be experienced sensually, perceived
empirically, and even studied scientifically. But since,
according to Moore, values are not natural properties,
insofar as they exist at all objectively it must be as
nonnatural properties.

How can values be understood other than in scant
negative terms? Moore would only say that they are
utterly simple, and that being utterly simple they are
undefinable. They are undefinable because they are
unanalyzable, and they are unanalyzable because, being
utterly simple, they are not composed of parts; parts,
of course, being an obvious precondition for any analysis.
Being wholly noncomplex there is nothing, and in
particular no collection of parts, with which values can
be correctly identified. Were someone to ask what had
value we could only reply honestly and truthfully, "What
had value!" Nothing more could be said and that would
be the end of the matter. Or again, if someone were to
ask how values could be defined, we could only reply
honestly and truthfully that they cannot be defined and
that would be that.

Given this circumstance one last question remains:
How are values to be known if not through experience,
and in particular, if not empirically through rigorous
and disciplined scientific inquiry? To this Moore, the
Intuitionist, had virtually nothing to say, other than
to repeat his own rather innocuous contention that known
values, or at least known basic values, are self-evident;
that is, that they are known by intuition. This is not
the same as firsthand experience, crude or common sense
phenomenal acquaintance, first impressions, or even
insight. Intuition is a form of direct or unmediated
perception. If values are nonnatural properties, they
cannot be known through experience, regardless of kind
or quality. They can only be known through a process--we
might call it an "a priori process"--that is not
restricted by empirical evidence.

By "self-evident" Moore meant something like
"immediately apprehended." While it might not be clear
exactly what this involves, it is easy enough to see that
as an epistemological process it has nothing to do with
empirical forms of knowledge, or for that matter even
with formal argumentation. What is legitimately
self-evident focuses on a substantive and transcendent
reality, and in this case, on values that represent
perfectly what philosophers since Immanuel Kant
(1724-1804) have called "synthetic-a priori truths."
If values are nonnatural properties, they can only be
known by nonempirical means, however this may be spelled
out in more specific and positive terms.

CRITICISMS OF INTUITIONISM
     Intuitionism began with the recognition that there
is an important distinction between descriptive and
prescriptive propositions. That judgments of value cannot
be reduced to judgments of fact is undeniable. But, as
Warnock contends, the account that intuitionism provides
of their differences is so barren as to be worse than
useless.

     [Intuitionism] seems deliberately, almost perversely,
     to answer no questions, to throw no light on any
     problem. One might almost say that the doctrine
     actually consists in a protracted denial that there
     is anything of the slightest interest to be said.
     The effect of this is worse than unhelpful: it is
     positively misleading.[4]

Within the context of intuitionism questions of value
are declared undiscussable. We are told that there is
something to be seen but nothing to be said. It is as
if the whole matter were all too obvious for words; and,
indeed, it is significant to point out that this doctrine
has usually appealed most to those who, like Moore, have
been least troubled by moral doubt. But however this
matter is viewed, the fact remains that the doctrine
itself is false and, to echo Warnock's sentiments, it
seems extraordinary that anyone would ever have actually
believed it was true.
     The reasons for this are plain enough. In the first
place, intuitionism grossly exaggerates the difference
between values and other kinds of facts. Values may be
different, but they are not all that different. Moore
made it look as if values were completely independent
of the rest of reality; "for all that he says," Warnock
complains, "the simple sui generis qualities of goodness
might quite well be detected as attaching to anything
whatever--alighting, so to speak, inexplicably and at
random upon anything, of whatever kind."[5] For Moore,
there is no reason why what is good is good; goodness
is a simple isolated quality, not just distinguishable
from, but entirely unrelated to, other objective

---

4. Warnock, Contemporary Moral Philosophy, pp. 12-13.
5. Ibid., p. 14.

properties. If this were actually true, values would not only be different from other kinds of facts, they would be objectively irrelevant to those facts. "The picture presented," Warnock continues, "is that of a realm of moral qualities, sui generis and indefinable, floating, as it were, quite free from anything else whatever, but cropping up here and there, quite contingently and for no reason, in bare conjunction with more ordinary features of the everyday world."[6]

If values are objective properties, they cannot be attached helter-skelter or haphazardly to anything whatever. They must be linked objectively to other aspects of our experience. Quoting Warnock once again, "they are not, as it were, stuck on objects or actions like postage stamps, quite indifferently to any other features of those objects or actions."[7] Values are dependent or consequential properties whose existence is both a cause and effect of other kinds of facts. Though Intuitionists have sometimes acknowledged this point, their theory has barred them from taking account of its significance.

A second reason for rejecting intuitionism is that it sheds no light on the problem of verifying prescriptive propositions. While Intuitionists believe that value statements are confirmable and, therefore, that prescriptive propositions can be established objectively as true or false, they provide no rational procedure for doing so. Instead they rely on immediate apprehension, a process so vaguely described as to be virtually unintelligible. Difficulties begin immediately once values are referred to as nonnatural properties. What exactly is a nonnatural property, and, in particular, what precisely would such a value consist in? Intuitionists are not able to answer these questions, and for this reason, have nothing to say about how value statements are verified, or can be known objectively to be true or false. Saying that values are undefinable, or that they can only be known directly, through intuition, is in Warnock's words, "worse than unhelpful: it is positively misleading."[8]

Moore claimed that statements of the form "X has value" are analogous in their fact-stating character to

---

6. Ibid., p. 14.
7. Ibid., p. 12.
8. Ibid., p. 13.

empirical statements such as "George has blue eyes." But we can establish the truth of this latter statement by "looking at the facts," in a quite literal sense. How can we establish the truth of statements of the form "X has value"? Certainly not through experience. If values are nonnatural properties, their presence or absence cannot be detected by anything like the ordinary methods and techniques of empirical investigation, no matter how sophisticated. Intuitionists are simply stuck with this dilemma. As for us, we are left without any means whatsoever for rationally resolving our differences in the perception of what is good or right.

Finally, we should mention the failure of intuitionism to account for the influence of values on conduct. If value predicates denote objective properties and value statements are purely descriptive, why should they have any special effect on what we do? According to intuitionism, knowing that something has value adds to our store of information. But what does it matter; why should we care? Presumably this knowledge differs from that which does not pertain to value. It provides us with a reason for adopting one course of action rather than another. Why the difference? Why should this information be relevant in our deciding what to do while, seemingly, other information is not? Once again we find that intuitionism is totally lacking an answer. Instead of explaining why knowledge of value has this special effect on what we choose or recommend, intuitionism is virtually silent. The influence of values on conduct appears, as Warnock says, "as a bare assumption, about which, as indeed about almost everything in the subject, there is nothing to be said."[9]

No theory can define its subject matter completely. Formal theories always assume the truth of certain postulates. Substantive theories always assume the existence of certain facts. While postulates and facts may be uniformly theory-dependent, while they may be invariably contingent upon one theory or another, any given theory, whether it be formal or substantive, must assume the truth of some postulate or the existence of some fact that is not totally a product of that theory. Thus, one of the goals of the theory is to help conceive, establish, and explain that postulate or fact. That values influence our lives and make a difference in the

---

9. Ibid., p. 16.

world as a whole is assumed by intuitionism as a fact. Yet, it remains a fact upon which no light whatsoever is thrown.

In retrospect, intuitionism seems like such a strange doctrine, "--a body of writing so acute and at the same time so totally unilluminating."[10]   One wonders how it could ever have been taken seriously. The idea that there is a vast corpus of objective values: first, related to other facts, but in ways we cannot explain; second, known, but we cannot say how; and third, overwhelmingly important for our conduct, but we cannot say why, is, to quote Warnock, "really astonishing."[11] It reflects an almost total absence of curiosity and emanates, we might guess, from an almost total lack of genuine doubt.

We seek to explain what we feel is in need of explanation. What seems obvious will not elicit thought. Because Intuitionist philosophers of the first part of this century were not generally beset by moral uncertainties, "what they called 'the facts' of morality were for them simply there, simply given, in the nature of things, standing in need from the theorist of nothing but clear recognition. . . . Why should room be left for uncertainty, if one does not feel any?"[12]   Where everything seems obvious, where we lack genuine doubt, the motive for inquiry is effectively squelched and could not be sustained even if it were to present itself.

---

10. Ibid., p. 16.
11. Ibid., p. 16.
12. Ibid., pp. 16, 17.

CHAPTER 5

EMOTIVISM AS A THEORY OF VALUE: THE EXTREMES OF NOMINALISM

The reaction against intuitionism was swift and devastating, and nowhere was it more extreme than in the case of emotivism. Emotivism, undoubtedly the most influential philosophical theory of value in this century, is best understood as a nominalistic reaction against formalism. Whereas formalism considers certain abstractions to be real, in the classical sense of being both objective and universal, nominalism regards all abstractions as unreal, as in and of themselves neither objective nor universal.

By equating values with nonnatural properties, formalism, of which intuitionism was but one manifestation, implied first, that values exist objectively and are not merely conceptions or ideas in someone's head; second, that values are nonnatural because they are universal; since, by definition, everything in nature is subject to change and since, also by definition, whatever is universal is unchangeable, values must be nonnatural, third, that values cannot be experienced literally, for experience rests on sense perception and the senses, again by definition, can only perceive natural properties; and thus, four, that in order to gain knowledge of values we must somehow transcend or go beyond our experience, we must adopt an a priori process of some kind such as intuition or pure reason. From the conviction that normative discourse cannot be <u>about</u> natural properties, Formalists, and Intuitionists in particular, concluded that it must be <u>about</u> properties that are nonnatural.

Emotivists rejected this analysis totally. They were among the first to suggest seriously and cogently

that normative discourse might not have any reference,
at least not any essential reference. While admitting
that the language of values is different from the language
of facts, that prescriptive propositions are of a
different class than descriptive propositions, they
regarded the difference as purely logical. Thus, it was
said that normative discourse is unique not because of
its subject matter, not because of what it is <u>about</u>,
but because of its peculiar conceptual structure. This
position is much more radical than the Intuitionist's
doctrine. The latter was designed merely to shift the
focus of discussion from natural to nonnatural properties.
Emotivists believed that there is nothing special about
the subject matter of normative discourse, that it owes
its distinctiveness to strictly formal features and,
therefore, can be <u>about</u> anything or nothing at all.

The basis of this belief was the positivistic
principle that meaningful propositions are either
empirically verifiable or analytic. From this it follows
that nonnatural properties are inconceivable and that
any theory that assumes they exist is utter nonsense.
Emotivism agrees with formalism in one respect, however.
Both insist that values cannot be defined in terms of
natural properties, which is to say that they cannot be
experienced and known through sense perception. But if
values cannot be conceived as nonnatural properties, nor
expressed as empirically verifiable propositions, they
must be subjective. This was precisely the reasoning
of emotivism. Normative discourse cannot be distinguished
by its subject matter if objectively it is content-free.

The Emotivist thesis was first put forth seriously
in a book by C. K. Ogden and I. A. Richards, <u>The Meaning
of Meaning</u>, published in 1923. The authors explicitly
criticized Moore's claim that the word "good" stands for
"a unique, unanalysable concept" that "is the subject-
matter of Ethics."

> This peculiar ethical use of "good" is, we suggest,
> a purely emotive use. When so used the word stands
> for nothing whatever, and has no symbolic function.
> Thus, when we so use it in the sentence, "<u>This
> is good</u>," we merely refer to <u>this</u>, and the addition
> of "is good" makes no difference whatever to our
> reference. When on the other hand, we say "<u>This
> is red</u>," the addition of "is red" to "this" does
> symbolize an extension of our reference, namely,

to some other red thing. But "is good" has no
comparable symbolic function; it serves only as
an emotive sign expressing our attitude to this,
and perhaps evoking similar attitudes in other
persons, or inciting them to actions of one kind
or another.[1]

In 1935 Rudolf Carnap, an original member of the
Vienna Circle, developed a variation of this thesis in
Philosophy and Logical Syntax:

The rule, "Do not kill," has grammatically the
imperative form and will therefore not be regarded
as an assertion. But the value statement, "Killing
is evil," although, like the rule, it is merely an
expression of a certain wish, has the grammatical
form of an assertive proposition. Most philosophers
have been deceived by this form into thinking that
a value statement is really an assertive proposition,
and must be either true or false. Therefore they
give reasons for their own value statements and try
to disprove those of their opponents. But actually
a value statement is nothing else than a command
in a misleading grammatical form. It may have
effects upon the actions of men, and these effects
may either be in accordance with our wishes or not;
but it is neither true nor false. It does not assert
anything and can neither by proved nor disproved.[2]

A book that appeared one year later, Language, Truth
and Logic by A. J. Ayer, served more than any other to

---

1. C. K. Ogden and I. A. Richards, The Meaning of Meaning
    (New York: Harcourt, Brace and World, 1923), p. 125.
    The reference to Moore is followed by a footnote:
    "Of course, if we define 'the good' as 'that of which
    we approve of approving,' or give any such definition
    when we say "This is good," we shall be making an
    assertion. It is only the indefinable 'good' which
    we suggest to be a purely emotive sign. The
    'something more' or 'something else' which, it is
    alleged, is not covered by any definition of 'good'
    is the emotional aura of the word."
2. Rudolf Carnap, Philosophy and Logical Syntax
    (London: Kegan Paul, Trench, Trubner, 1935), p. 24.

convey this message to the educated public. He wrote
that normative discourse "has no factual meaning" and
that, therefore, prescriptive propositions, like "Stealing
money is wrong," are neither true nor false.

> It is as if I had written "Stealing money!!"--where
> the shape and thickness of the exclamation marks
> show, by a suitable convention, that a special sort
> of moral disapproval is the feeling which is being
> expressed. It is clear that there is nothing said
> here which can be true or false. Another man may
> disagree with me about the wrongness of stealing,
> in the sense that he may not have the same feelings
> about stealing as I have, and he may quarrel with
> me on account of my moral sentiments. But he cannot,
> strictly speaking, contradict me. For in saying
> that a certain type of action is right or wrong,
> I am not making a factual statement, not even a
> statement about my own state of mind. I am merely
> expressing certain moral sentiments. And the man
> who is ostensibly contradicting me is merely
> expressing his moral sentiments. So that there is
> plainly no sense in asking which of us is in the
> right. For neither of us is asserting a genuine
> proposition.[3]

Ayer was willing to go so far as to say that we may
define ethical words in terms of "the different responses
which they are calculated to provoke" as well as in terms
of "the different feelings they are ordinarily taken to
express." "But in every case in which one would commonly
be said to be making an ethical judgment, the function
of the relevant ethical word is purely 'emotive.'"[4]

Notwithstanding these early contributions, it was
left to C. L. Stevenson to work out the logic of
emotivism. With the publication of Ethics and Language
in 1944, this task was essentially completed. Seen in
conjunction with other articles he has written before
and since, it expands the basic idea of emotivism into
a full-fledged philosophical standpoint and shows the

3. A. J. Ayer, Language, Truth and Logic (London: Victor
    Gollancz, Ltd., 1936), p. 159. (Available currently
    in 1952 Dover edition.)
4. Ibid., pp. 160-61.

extent to which nominalism can sustain a critique of substantive theories of value.

The book begins by discussing the nature of ethical disagreement. Agreement is treated "mainly by implication," not only for the sake of "expository economy," but because disagreement presents "instances where methods of reasoning are more overtly employed, and more readily available for illustration and study."[5] The question is precisely this: Is ethical disagreement "parallel to that found in the natural sciences, differing only with regard to the relevant subject matter; or is it of some broadly different sort?"[6]

Stevenson argued the latter. When he compared disputes over matters of fact, which is what concerns the natural sciences, with disputes over values, which is what concerns ethics, he found that cases of the first kind resulted from disagreement in belief, whereas cases of the second kind resulted from disagreement in attitude. There is disagreement in belief whenever Mr. A believes p and Mr. B believes not-p, or something incompatible with p, and neither is content to let the belief of the other remain unchallenged.[7] A disagreement in attitude occurs whenever Mr. A has a favorable attitude toward something and Mr. B has an unfavorable or less favorable attitude toward it and neither is content to let the other's attitude remain unchanged.[8]

The difference is essentially this: disagreement in belief involves opposition of beliefs both of which cannot be true. Disagreement in attitude involves opposition of attitudes both of which cannot be

---

5. C. L. Stevenson, Ethics and Language (New Haven: Yale Univ. Press, 1944), p. 5. See also in this regard, "The Nature of Ethical Disagreement," Facts and Values--Studies in Ethical Analysis (New Haven: Yale Univ. Press, 1963), pp. 1-9.
6. Ibid., p. 2.
7. Stevenson does not explicitly define "belief." But the implication is clearly that it is a formal or substantive proposition supposed to be true.
8. Both formulations appear in Stevenson's "The Nature of Ethical Disagreement," Facts and Values--Studies in Ethical Analysis, p. 1. See also in this regard, Stevenson, Ethics and Language, pp. 3-4.

satisfied.[9] The reduction of disputes over values to
opposing attitudes was supported by Stevenson with two
observations: first, that attitudes determine the beliefs
that are relevant to such disputes; and second, that these
disputes usually terminate even when disagreement in
belief still lingers.[10]

If we suppose these observations to be correct, the
intention of normative discourse is not primarily to
convey information or influence our beliefs. While it
may do so incidentally, these functions are far from
indispensable. The intention of normative discourse is
to express and influence our attitudes, and to the extent
that our attitudes are manifested in our actions, to
affect our conduct as well. "Broadly speaking," Stevenson
declared, "there are two different purposes which lead
us to use language."

> On the one hand we use words (as in science) to
> record, clarify, and communicate beliefs. On the
> other hand we use words to give vent to our feelings
> (interjections), or to create moods (poetry), or
> to incite people to actions or attitudes
> (oratory).[11]

The first use of words he called "descriptive," the
second, "dynamic."[12] Normative discourse is defined
precisely by this latter purpose.

Moore had a vague understanding of this purpose when
he said that values cannot be identified except with

---

9. Ibid., p. 2.
10. Stevenson, "The Nature of Ethical Disagreement,"
    Facts and Values--Studies in Ethical Analysis,
    pp. 4-5. See also in this regard, Stevenson, Ethics
    and Language, pp. 14-15.
11. Stevenson, "The Emotive Meaning of Ethical Terms,"
    Facts and Values--Studies in Ethical Analysis,
    p. 18.
12. On Stevenson's analysis, this distinction is totally
    subjective, for it "depends solely upon the purposes
    of the speaker." (Ibid., p. 19.) If these
    purposes were not also conceived as existing solely
    in the mind of the speaker, as purely formal or
    nonsubstantive, this conclusion could have been
    avoided.

themselves, nor expressed in anything but their own
terms. But this insight was skewed by his addiction to
a referential theory of meaning. That is, he began by
presuming that intelligible ideas and significant
propositions must denote actually existing facts. This
led him to posit peculiar (because unique) nonnatural
properties as referents for the language of values.
Stevenson considered this to be a serious mistake, for
it assumes that normative discourse functions primarily
with a descriptive purpose. On the analysis he proposed,
prescriptive propositions may describe an antecedently
existing reality, but need not necessarily. The
descriptive content of these propositions can be altered
or removed altogether without changing their essential
character. As Moore's case so aptly demonstrates, the
influence of values on conduct will appear utterly
mysterious so long as this truth goes undetected.

If intelligible ideas and significant propositions
were limited to those that denote actually existing facts,
as Moore supposed, then language could have but one
purpose--to describe or provide information. That
language can also have a dynamic purpose shows the
fundamental error in any referential theory of meaning.
Stevenson concluded from this that when language is used
descriptively it has descriptive meaning. But when
it is used dynamically it has emotive meaning. Each
type of meaning was assumed to represent a distinct
category, the former being concerned with the objective
realm and the latter with the province of subjectivity.
In actual practice language can be used in ways that are
simultaneously descriptive and emotive. But as the
objective realm and the province of subjectivity are
separable ontologically; descriptive and emotive meaning
are distinguishable conceptually.

Thus, for Stevenson, the unique features of normative
discourse were rooted in the most fundamental of
philosophical considerations. They symbolize a special
kind of meaning. Value terms are defined by their dynamic
use. They allow us to express our feelings and to
persuade others to share our attitudes. Justifications
of value judgments can be similarly characterized. In
a sense they are not judgments at all, but rather emotive
expressions of language directed by a dynamic purpose.
Their sole criterion for success is effectiveness in
serving as means towards a prescribed end. If they yield
the results intended, they are warranted. Otherwise they

are unwarranted. We cannot ask, in a literal sense, if
they are valid or sound, but only if they produce the
desired convictions in the appropriate person or group.
    Given this viewpoint, moral arguments have more in
common with advertising, propaganda, and even intimidation
than we might ordinarily suspect. They surely have little
to do with the standard forms of argumentation. They
are distinguished by their function, by the results they
seek to obtain, precisely in the manner of nonrational
modes of communication, not by their content. Whether
they are good or bad arguments on logical or rational
grounds is clearly beside the point.
    Emotivism did away with many of the problems that
had been perpetuated by intuitionism. Most importantly,
it made no claims for the existence of mysterious
nonnatural properties. Indeed, the existence of
nonnatural properties was explicitly denied. Furthermore,
where intuitionism could not account for the influence
of values on conduct, emotivism defined normative
discourse by its dynamic purpose. But however we view
these issues, the truth is that emotivism is a false
doctrine. It perpetrated errors of its own which have
proven to be no less disastrous than those committed by
intuitionism. To these errors we now turn.

CRITICISMS OF EMOTIVISM
    When emotivism first appeared as a full-fledged
theory of value, it looked invincible. But as
philosophers began to examine it more closely serious
shortcomings became evident. Basically, emotivism
overplays the fact, undeniable in itself, that normative
discourse has a dynamic purpose. Obviously, value
judgments are designed to influence our conduct. Moral
judgments, in particular, aim to encourage certain
activities and discourage others. Nevertheless, emotivism
fails to analyze correctly the ways in which these
judgments actually work. Essentially this is Warnock's
position:

        while . . . intuitionism offers no intelligible
        account of the relation between moral judgment and
        conduct, the emotivist thesis connects moral judgment
        with conduct in a perfectly intelligible and (within
        limits) clear and definite manner. Unfortunately,
        . . . this connection, while possessing the merit

of being intelligible, clear, and definite, has the
demerit also of being completely wrong, and indeed,
in a certain sense, disastrously wrong.[13]

The reason Warnock believes emotivism to be, "in
a certain sense, disastrously wrong" is that it not only
fails to provide a correct analysis of the ways in which
value judgments actually work, but "more damagingly, it
positively misassimilates those ways to those of such
purely manipulative procedures as propaganda, emotional
bullying, brain-washing, and the hard sell. We ask how
moral discourse is different; we are told that it is
not."[14]

Where Moore paid little or no attention to the
dynamic use of language, asking only what normative
discourse is about, Stevenson erred in the opposite
direction. He virtually ignored the descriptive use of
language in prescriptive propositions and asked only what
normative discourse is for. That value judgments are
designed to influence our conduct is true enough. But
we need to recognize limiting considerations.

To begin with, Stevenson's conception of attitudes
is almost wholly mistaken. He equated attitudes with
feelings, such that a change in one was synonymous with
a change in the other. But my expressing my disapproval
is not the same as giving vent to my feelings. And my
seeking to change your attitude involves more than seeking
to change how you feel. Particular feelings usually
accompany specific attitudes, but normally they are not
the sole or even primary determinants of these attitudes.
In a penetrating critique of Stevenson's Ethics and
Language, J. O. Urmson, who is basically sympathetic
with Stevenson, writes:

to ascribe to a person a certain attitude is to
ascribe to him a certain pattern of thoughts,
beliefs, feelings, emotions, words and deeds, and
the relative importance of the various elements in
the pattern will vary according to the particular
character of the attitude. So long as the pattern
continues to be manifested in his activities when

13. G. J. Warnock, Contemporary Moral Philosophy (New
     York: Macmillan, 1967), p. 24.
14. Ibid., p. 74.

circumstances are appropriate, so long does the attitude last.[15]

On this rendering, Stevenson was wrong to identify attitudes with feelings, and equally mistaken to talk about attitudes as logically distinct from beliefs. An attitude is virtually synonymous with "conduct," in the fullest sense of the term. It represents a whole array of feelings, emotions, beliefs, and behavior that have been integrated into a more or less consistent pattern of action, or what might be thought of alternatively as a "personality." The relative importance of the different elements within the pattern varies according to the character of the attitude. But in order to possess the attitude one must display the pattern, or project this personality, whenever the situation warrants.

This datum of experience has an obvious bearing on Stevenson's conception of changing attitudes. A change in attitude requires more than a change in feeling. It requires modification of the entire system within which persons feel, think, and behave—in short, their conduct or personality. Feelings are only one of the factors that determine attitudes, and are always a factor that can be outweighed by others. Truly, there are times when an emphasis on feeling, or any significant show of emotion would be absurdly out of place. "Thus," to use Urmson's example, "one may evaluate one type of power shovel or insecticide more highly than another; if someone disagrees with us we shall have a case of disagreement in attitude. But we should appear ridiculous if we were to allow our disagreement to become in any way emotional; only a fanatic will feel emotionally committed to a design for power shovels."[16]

A perceptible change in any of the components that constitute our action may alter the pattern that defines our attitude. But it does not necessarily dissolve our attitude. Up to a point at least, we can alter our feelings, just as we can alter our thoughts or behavior, and still retain the same attitude.

Attitudes and feelings differ in other ways too. We can decide on our attitudes, but our feelings leave little room for choice. Once again quoting Urmson,

---

15. U. O. Urmson, The Emotive Theory of Ethics (New York: Oxford Univ. Press, 1969), p. 43.
16. Ibid., p. 45.

our emotions are relatively beyond our control,
completely so in the case of the less stable among
us. We may try to suppress them, to discipline
ourselves in ways which we expect to modify them,
or to have them modified for us by psychotherapists;
but we cannot simply choose which emotions to feel.
We can, however, choose our words and our deeds,
or most of us can most of the time. Because of this
we can to a great extent choose our attitudes and
thus be immediately responsible for them,
particularly those attitudes to which word and deed
are of paramount importance.[17]

This is precisely the reason we speak so naturally
of people adopting and maintaining attitudes, of their
accepting or rejecting them intelligently, of attitudes
being more or less judicious and reasonable. But we do
not adopt or maintain feelings, nor do we accept or reject
them intelligently; though they may be appropriate or
inappropriate, they can hardly be judicious or reasonable.
Similarly, as Urmson points out, we can speak quite
naturally of disagreement in attitude, just as we speak
of disagreement in belief, but we do not disagree in
feeling.

We can call certain differences in attitude
disagreements precisely because we can maintain
attitudes as we maintain beliefs, because we can
be argued out of attitudes as we can be argued out
of beliefs, because with reason given we can be
expected to abandon attitudes as with reason given
we can be expected to abandon beliefs. But we
cannot, and do not, speak of disagreement in emotion
or feeling precisely because we do not maintain
emotions and feelings and cannot be argued out of
them.[18]

Rather than speaking of disagreement in feeling,
we need to speak instead of emotional incompatibility
or disharmony. Where disharmony results in a serious
problem we might resolve to see a psychiatrist or seek
advice from friends on how to surmount, mitigate, or live
with this condition; "but we cannot be argued out of it,

17.   Ibid., p. 43.
18.   Ibid., pp. 43-44.

even if we may choose to maintain a sensible attitude
towards it and towards each other, in spite of it."[19]
     If Stevenson had wanted to distinguish feelings and
beliefs, he could have done so easily. Although the two
are obviously related their conceptual overlap is minimal
enough to justify each as a separate idea. The truth
is, however, that this distinction would not have been
of much use in Stevenson's analysis of normative terms.
He needed the distinction between attitudes and beliefs.
But, as we have seen, this latter distinction is much
more problematic. Beliefs are essential components of
attitudes. If they are inextricably bound together
conceptually, it is impossible to separate disagreement
in _attitude_ and disagreement in _belief_ in the manner
Stevenson specified. Intelligence can be as suitable
for one as for the other. We might adopt or abandon
attitudes for the same reasons we adopt or abandon
beliefs.
     Why were Emotivists unable to see this point?
Warnock believes there were two reasons. First, they
were overimpressed with the idea that normative discourse
has a purpose. While Intuitionists admittedly ignored
this fact, Emotivists seemed to concentrate on it to the
exclusion of all others. They asked only what normative
discourse is _for_, and "scarcely raised seriously the
question what it actually is."[20] That normative
discourse is designed to influence attitudes is
incontrovertible, but exactly how is a matter that
Emotivists plainly failed to understand. John Dewey
voiced a similar complaint. In reviewing _Ethics and
Language_ he criticized Stevenson's analysis for reducing
"ethical sentences" to subjective preferences.

> One can agree fully that ethical sentences (as far
> as their end and use is concerned) "plead and advise"
> and speak "to the conative-affective natures of men"
> [_Ethics and Language_, p. 13]. Their use and intent
> is practical. But the point at issue concerns the
> means by which this result is accomplished. It is
> . . . a radical fallacy to convert the end-in-view
> into an inherent constituent of the means by which,
> in genuinely moral sentences, the end is

19. Ibid., p. 44.
20. Warnock, _Contemporary Moral Philosophy_, pp. 28-29.

accomplished. To take the cases in which "emotional" factors accompany the giving of reasons as if this accompaniment factor were an inherent part of the judgment is, I submit, both a theoretical error and is, when widely adopted in practice, a source of moral weakness.[21]

Dewey is only suggesting here what Warnock states explicitly: that insofar as Emotivists actually discussed the problem of how normative discourse influences attitudes, they were seriously mistaken.

Their basic error was to equate attitudes with feelings. As a consequence, if, for example, I expressed my disapproval, it would be identified with the widely different phenomenon of "giving vent" to my feelings; and if I sought to change your attitude, it would be interpreted fundamentally as an attempt to change your emotions. Under such circumstances must it not be the case that my language is emotive and has primarily emotive meaning? Hence, the conclusion that normative discourse and the value judgments it generates are "essentially non-rational, a matter not of argument but of psychological pressure, not of reasons but of efficacious manipulation."[22]

What Emotivists called "emotive meaning" is referred to more accurately as emotive influence. The difference parallels that between the design of language and the consequences of its use. In an essay on logical empiricism and value judgments, Abraham Kaplan provides a nice illustration of this point:

The shock effect of certain words . . . is not meant by them, but is produced by what is meant--or, more accurately, is produced by the utterance of words

---

21.   John Dewey, "Ethical Subject-Matter and Language," Journal of Philosophy, 52(26)(December 1945), 702-3. Dewey adds in a footnote on the bottom of p. 703, "I would not overemphasize the matter, but I get the impression that Stevenson is influenced at times in connection with the "meaning" of moral judgments, by that ambiguity in which "meaning" has the sense of both design or purpose and that which a sign indicates." [My emphasis]
22.   Warnock, Contemporary Moral Philosophy, p. 29.

with a certain meaning. That a statement is
shocking, and even habitually and characteristically
so, does not compel the analysis that it somehow
"means" the shock.[23]

The effect of an utterance can have a significant impact
on its meaning, but it does not by itself define its
meaning. Yet, this is exactly the claim of emotivism,
that normative words, words that speak to the value or
worth of things, are causes that mean their effects.
This blunder led many to reject emotivism out of hand.
For others, however, the problem was to correct
emotivism's theory of meaning without abandoning its
nominalistic assumptions. Of the work done in this latter
tradition, prescriptivism stands out as the most
successful. If only for this reason, it deserves our
serious and respectful examination.

---

23. Abraham Kaplan, "Logical Empiricism and Value
    Judgments," The Philosophy of Rudolf Carnap, ed.
    Paul A. Schilpp, c copyright The Library of Living
    Philosophers, Inc. (LaSalle, Ill.: Open Court,
    1963), p. 830.

CHAPTER 6

PRESCRIPTIVISM AS A THEORY OF VALUE: AN AMENDMENT TO EMOTIVISM

Prescriptivism is best seen as an attempt to correct the more glaring errors of emotivism without abandoning its basic posture. Both are nominalistic and, therefore, both maintain that values are inherently subjective. Neither sees the descriptive function of normative discourse as primary and therefore neither regards facts as essential preconditions for value judgments.

Still, there are important differences. Emotivism contends that normative discourse and judgments of value are designed to influence conduct through emotional persuasion. Prescriptivism holds, more modestly, that this kind of linguistic behavior is intended merely to provide guidance. Rather than aiming to manipulate conduct, as supposed by Emotivists, normative discourse and judgments of value are to be understood from this second perspective as giving counsel. As Prescriptivists will be quick to point out, emotivism does not distinguish between my telling you what to do, on the one hand; and on the other hand, the effects or consequences, actual or intended, of my telling you what to do. For precisely this reason emotivism can only recognize one alternative to the descriptive use of language.

Prescriptivism relies heavily on the work of J. L. Austin who contended that words allow us to do many different kinds of things. Most generally they allow us first, to make meaningful verbal or written gestures; second, to say things that have a distinct logical force; and third, to produce certain effects within our environment. Austin considered each of these uses of language as a unique type of linguistic performance or "act."[1] The first he called a "locutionary act," the second an "illocutionary act," and the third a "perlocutionary act."

Illocutionary acts were shown to be especially important in understanding the workings of language. They define the intent of its use. In performing an illocutionary act we can formulate a conception, describe a fact, ask a question, issue a command, make a promise, condemn an action, confess a transgression, express resolve, offer advice, give praise, implore mercy, exhort compliance, and so on and on. The point is that these acts cannot be understood solely as meaningful verbal or written gestures. They need to be distinguished from each other as well as from the effects they produce. Not only has the special character of illocutionary acts frequently gone unnoticed but the role of illocutionary acts in determining meaning has rarely, if ever, been fully appreciated.

Meaningful propositions are defined by their illocutionary force. They may or may not have a reference and they may or may not produce experienceable consequences. What is essential is that they represent actions that can be understood logically. Intuitionism assumes that meaning is a matter of reference. Yet, some meaningful propositions have no reference. That seven angels can dance on the head of a pin, for instance, might be categorically false. Still, for all that, the proposition is no less intelligible.

Similarly, emotivism is mistaken to suggest that there is a special kind of meaning that is totally subjective. Maintaining, as emotivism does, that prescriptive propositions have meaning because of their natural power or disposition to produce or be produced by particular mental states or "feelings," is itself a prescriptive proposition. To regard the distinction between sense and nonsense as purely psychological does not represent a discovery, theoretical or otherwise, of the standard of meaning actually used when making normative pronouncements. Rather, it proclaims the standard to be "causal efficacy" and thereby stipulates how normative pronouncements ought to be interpreted.

---

1. See in this regard J. L. Austin, How To Do Things with Words (New York: Oxford Univ. Press, 1965).

The problem with emotivism is that it defines normative pronouncements by their perlocutionary force, and this cannot account for their meaning as it is actually found in ordinary language. Emotivism is proposed as a scientific or substantive philosophical theory where the primary concern is its correspondence to an existential reality. It is not proposed as a normative theory, or as a theory of pure logic where the primary concern is with internal consistency, that is, with the consistency of ideas within the theory itself. As a scientific or substantive philosophical theory, emotivism must acknowledge that there are at least some facts pertaining to the theory that exist independently of the theory. All the facts pertinent to the theory may be assumed to be theory dependent, but not all these facts can be assumed to depend on the same theory. A scientific or substantive philosophical theory cannot create its subject matter completely.

By following Austin's lead, prescriptivism purports to be neither normative, nor purely logical, nor inaccurate as a scientific or substantive philosophical theory. The distinction between meaningful and meaningless propositions is not regarded as a matter of reference, or a question of emotions, but rather as a function of linguistic conventions. Meaning is believed to arise from rules of communication established either universally or within a particular group of language users. Meaningful propositions are constructed in accordance with these rules, meaningless ones are not.

Armed with this analysis of meaning, prescriptivism is believed by its supporters to account objectively for the facts of normative discourse and to represent both a sound theory of value and a rationally credible moral philosophy. Although in many ways an improvement over what had come before, and although it has had the effect of fortifying the metaphysical thesis of nominalism, prescriptivism is still fundamentally deficient. To see why, we must examine the work of R. M. Hare, prescriptivism's most notable proponent.

In The Language of Morals, published in 1952, and in a later book, Freedom and Reason, published in 1963, Hare claimed that normative discourse has two essential features: it always implies imperatives, and the imperatives it implies have the quality of being

universal, that is, they are universalizable by design.[2]
     Precisely what does it mean to "imply an imperative"?
Most simply put, it means that were I to issue an
imperative I would be telling you, by implication, to
do something. Notice that I would be performing an
illocutionary act, not a perlocutionary act. In issuing
the imperative I am merely telling you what to do.
Whether you actually do what I say is another matter
entirely. What it means to "accept" an imperative is
similarly simple to state. It means to act in accordance
with the imperative. If prescriptive propositions imply
imperatives, and accepting an imperative implies acting
on that imperative, then accepting a prescriptive
proposition also implies acting on that proposition.
     We need to keep in mind, as Hare certainly did, that
accepting an imperative involves a logical commitment,
but not a causal relationship. It does not move one to
act necessarily as the imperative implies. Rather it
obligates one conceptually to view acceptance in
particular terms.[3] Inasmuch as issuing an imperative
amounts to telling someone what to do, acceptance is a
question of doing it and rejection is a question of not
doing it. We should also point out that owing to the
same factors one is constrained by rationality from giving
out conflicting imperatives. Unless the conflict is
unreal, as in the case where imperatives are issued under
radically different circumstances, sound logic demands
that at least one of these imperatives be withdrawn.
An imperative functions as a reason, not a cause, and
has as much to do with the justification of conduct as
with the explanation of it.
     We can speak here of "justification" in any number
of ways, but basically there are two: "justification"
in the sense of establishing the existence of conduct
as a fact, or at least of establishing our knowledge of
its existence, and "justification" in the sense of
establishing the propriety of conduct.
     In the first instance, "justification" involves the
conception and description of conduct as well as

---

2. R. M. Hare, The Language of Morals (Oxford: Clarendon
    Press, 1952) and Freedom and Reason (Oxford:
    Clarendon Press, 1963).
3. G. J. Warnock, Contemporary Moral Philosophy (New
    York: Macmillan, 1967), pp. 32-33.

establishing the existence of the fact, or, more modestly, our knowledge of its existence, in the narrow sense of "proving" or verifying its being as an antecedent and independent reality. The imperative helps create or define the fact, instilling it with meaning and significance. And, it represents a defense of the factual judgment that the event actually took place, that the reality occurred as an institutional fact. In the second case, "justification" focuses on the normative or moral status of the fact. The imperative provides the basis for the value judgment that the conduct was right or obligatory.

Hare hastened to add an important qualification in all this which brought into consideration what he believed to be the second essential feature of normative discourse. Although prescriptive propositions imply imperatives, not all imperatives are prescriptive. In the standard sense, prescriptive propositions are established in law.

Immanuel Kant recognized this fact in his conception of a categorical imperative. A categorical imperative, as contrasted with a hypothetical imperative, is unconditionally and universally binding. It is true for everyone, without exception. As Hare put this point:

> in making up my mind what I ought to do . . . I have to ask myself "What maxim (to use Kant's term) can I accept as of universal application in cases like this, whether or not I play the part in the situation which I am playing now?"[4]

An imperative standing alone cannot be generalized. Telling someone what to do does not in itself imply a future commitment, or a commitment to tell others similarly situated to do likewise. It is limited to a precise time and place and requires no assumption of norms.

A prescriptive proposition, however, requires just this. It is tied logically to distinguishable features of the situation. What this means is that any situation sharing in these features is regulated by the same demand. In other words, a prescriptive proposition implies the same imperative for every situation of that kind. We are constrained conceptually from accepting

---

4. Hare, Freedom and Reason, p. 72.

the proposition as anything less than a matter of
principle. In terms of standards this means that
committing myself in one instance is tantamount to
committing myself in every instance.

CRITICISMS OF PRESCRIPTIVISM
    To say normative discourse is prescriptive (in Hare's
sense), as to say it is emotive (in Stevenson's sense),
is neither true nor distinctive. That normative discourse
is designed to influence conduct is indisputable. Only,
the point is that, in explaining this influence,
prescriptivism, like emotivism, is seriously mistaken.
    Prescriptive propositions relate to behavior in a
manner far more complex than prescriptivism would lead
us to believe. Hare tried to undermine this criticism
by pointing out that prescriptive propositions can be
understood as a genus as well as a specie of a
genus.[5] In the latter case, prescribing is set in
juxtaposition with such speech acts as praising,
condemning, imploring, persuading, and exhorting. It
means, as distinct from these things, giving counsel or
providing advice. Hence, while representing a category
which itself has members, or instances, it serves as
a member of a larger family of speech acts all of which
have the same or at least a similar degree of abstractness
and generality. In the former case, however, prescribing
is of a higher order. It designates the whole of this
larger family. Relative to individual family members
it is more abstract and more general. By means of this
measure, prescribing defines a category, or type of speech
act that includes praising, condemning, advising, and
so forth, as different forms of the same classification.
    Thus conceived, prescribing is a multidimensional,
many-faceted process which, when fully understood, tells
us a great deal about the complex ways in which normative
discourse relates to behavior. But how to understand
this process? According to Hare, the "right strategy"
is to study its form and, in particular, to study "the
formal properties of the word 'ought.'"[6] He said this

---

5.   R. M. Hare, "Review of Warnock's Contemporary Moral
     Philosophy," Mind, 77(July 1968), 438.
6.   Ibid., p. 437.

because he believed that "moral words are best understood
by examining certain central uses of them, and explaining
the rest indirectly by reference to these."[7]
What Hare concluded was:

> one of the essential features of these central
> uses is a feature, namely the possibility of deeds
> being consonant or dissonant with words, which
> imperatives also have, and which puts them both in
> the genus "prescription," though differentiated as
> species by the fact that moral judgments are
> universalizable and imperatives not.[8]

One rather bizarre consequence of this view is that
moral philosophy, like normative discourse generally,
amounts to little more than an a priori exercise.
Inasmuch as prescriptive propositions are defined
exclusively by their logical properties, nothing remains
for philosophy except to work out their implications.
Hence, knowing that prescriptive propositions imply
imperatives and that accepting an imperative implies doing
what it says, we can argue in the reverse order that
acting as an imperative decrees is tantamount to accepting
the imperative and that this in turn is equivalent to
accepting any prescription that implies that imperative.
     This thesis, that our moral principles are revealed
in what we do, is inherent in prescriptivism. But, as
Warnock has demonstrated, there are counterexamples.[9]
In the first place, we might not have any principles; "a
man may . . . be so changeable, volatile, whimsical, and
inconsistent that he could not be said to hold--and
perhaps, for what it is worth, he does not even profess--
any principles at all."[10] Where conduct reveals neither
patterns nor regularities, no principles exist.
     In the second place, we might have principles, but
not moral principles. Not all principles are moral
principles, nor are principles moral merely because they
influence what we do. A thoroughgoing egoist, for
instance, might act on principles of self-regarding

---

7. Ibid., p. 439.
8. Ibid., p. 439.
9. Warnock, Contemporary Moral Philosophy, pp. 48-52.
10. Ibid., pp. 48-49.

prudence, but these would not be moral principles. His
behavior might reveal his principles, but not his moral
principles.

In the third place, we might have moral principles,
yet for one reason or another not act on them. Why?
Perhaps because we were weak-willed or neglectful. Or
perhaps because we considered other things to be more
important. Be this as it may, to insist that we cannot
hold moral principles without "doing what they say" is,
to use Warnock's term, "overrigorous."

> It may be the case that a man who never, or hardly
> ever, acts as some principle requires cannot be
> regarded as sincere in his profession of subscription
> to the principle. But between total non-acceptance
> and unvarying compliance there are many intermediate
> cases: a man may act in breach of a principle in
> many different styles or manners, and may view his
> lapses with many different shades of regret,
> self-criticism, or remorse. Surely not every
> voluntary fall from virtue condemns every virtuous
> profession as insincere.[11]

If accepting a prescriptive proposition is not inevitably
synonymous with acting as an imperative implies, then
prescriptive propositions need not always imply
imperatives, and prescriptivism will leave something to
be desired as a philosophical interpretation of the
language of values.

RATIONALITY AS A LOGICAL STIPULATION

Even though mistaken in its emphasis on imperatives
in normative discourse, prescriptivism might be seen as
correct on another matter of far greater importance.
For does it not say that prescriptive propositions can
be supported by reason? And is this not a fact that any
credible theory of value must duly recognize?
Intuitionism was rejected because it substitutes for
reason nondiscursive modes of knowing. Emotivism was
rejected because it regards reason as irrelevant, except
as a strategy for achieving predetermined and subjectively
defined goals.

---

11. Ibid., p. 51.

When compared with either of these alternatives, prescriptivism is an obvious improvement. Reason is acknowledged as a factor in both the formulation and appraisal of value judgments. Prescriptive propositions are neither conceived nor judged solely by their effectiveness. Rather they are viewed as having a logic of their own, independent of their dynamic purpose or actual effects. With this analysis, prescriptions are not so much action-causing as action-guiding, making it appropriate to ask for, and deliberate about their objective justification. I might be right in telling you what to do even though you reject my advice, or wrong even though you accept it.

The question is: Does this concession go far enough? Does prescriptivism really bring value judgments within the scope of rationality? What it says is that anyone who affirms a prescriptive proposition is logically bound to apply the same standards in every situation of that kind. As Warnock put it:

> For me to assert that you ought not to do X in situation Y commits me, as a matter of logic, to the general "principle" that no one should do things like X in situations like Y--"like" meaning here "not relevantly distinguishable from." Generality of this sort is implicit in all moral judgment.[12]

But solely on the basis of this requirement what is there to rationally argue about? Precisely what might be at issue? We might debate the conceptual consequences of how standards are being used, whether they are being applied consistently. But we cannot argue rationally over the standards themselves.

The creation of standards remains as arbitrary on Hare's analysis as on Stevenson's. Substantive questions that surround the formation and defense of standards continue to be seen as subjective. While evaluations can be established objectively, valuations cannot. The principle of universalizability is an acknowledgement of some degree of objectivity in the justification of value judgments. Unfortunately it applies only to the form of these arguments. Their content remains virtually unchecked.

---

12. *Ibid.*, p. 43.

This is why the principle of universalizability "does not, as a weapon of moral argument, carry much firepower."[13] It cannot set limits on the rational choice of standards other than logical limits. Anything can serve as a rational standard so long as it is conceivable and consistently maintained. The ethical sense of "can" is here equivalent to the logical sense. Or to put it somewhat differently, what is logically possible is taken to be ethically possible. If what we do is logically comprehensible, that is, intelligible and without logical contradiction, then on this view we cannot be morally constrained. Where our actions are clear and consistent no one has reason to disapprove. But is this not tantamount to saying that substantively our standards are arbitrary?

In this we have the most serious objection to prescriptivism as a theory of value. If asked to justify my standards, all I can do in the way of reason-giving is to say that they are implied by my prescriptions. But, of course, these are my prescriptions and, as Warnock writes:

> what are reasons for me, are, for you, not only not necessarily good reasons, but possibly not reasons at all. And thus, what we speak of as argument between two parties emerges essentially as nothing more than the articulation by each of his own position. For you to say that my view is wrong is to say only that your position excludes that view; for me to "argue" that my view is right is to show only that my position includes it. And there is nothing else, on this view, that argument can do; for there are no "reasons" that either party can appeal to independently of, and so genuinely in support of, his own prescriptions.[14]

The only thing we can really argue about is consistency. Where I could demonstrate this, my actions would have all the reason you could ever require, unless, that is, you rejected my prescriptions. In that case, they would have all the reason that I could ever require,

---

13. Ibid., p. 46.
14. Ibid., p. 46.

even though for you, perhaps, they would be the epitome of irrationality.

It would be foolish to suggest that questions of value can be settled in anything like the definite manner of a proof. If the experience of life shows us anything, it is that controversies over the value or worth of things can rarely, if ever, be resolved with rational certainty. Even when we exercise the best judgment possible, our opinions are likely to remain no more than articles of faith. It may seem that prescriptivism says no more than this. But as Warnock demonstrates, it actually says much more. It says:

> not only that it is for us to decide what our moral opinions are, but also that it is for us to decide what to take as grounds for or against any moral opinion. We are not only, as it were, free to decide on the evidence, but also free to decide what evidence is. I do not, it seems, decide that flogging is wrong because I am against cruelty; rather, I decide that flogging is wrong because I decide to be against cruelty. And what, if I did make that decision, would be my ground for making it? That I am opposed to the deliberate infliction of pain? No—rather that I decide to be opposed to it. And so on.[15]

No doubt there are people who form and defend their opinions precisely in this way--who, we might say, not only make up their own minds, but make up their own evidence too. "But such a person, surely, is not so much a model as a menace; not an examplar of moral reasoning, but a total abstainer from any serious concern with reason."[16] If values were simply a matter of choice, the valuation process would be hopelessly irrational. Can we show it to be otherwise? Now is the time to try, even if it is too much to expect that we will be able to say everything that needs to be said.

---

15. Ibid., p. 47.
16. Ibid., p. 47.

JUSTIFYING JUDGMENTS OF VALUE: A FOURTH REPLY REVISITED

We have come full circle in our consideration of value theories. We began with intuitionism which said that normative discourse cannot be <u>about</u> natural properties, and so must be <u>about</u> nonnatural properties. Criticizing this view, Emotivists argued that normative discourse cannot be <u>about</u> nonnatural properties either. Indeed, they said that objectively normative discourse is content-free, that it has no reference, at least no essential reference.

According to Stevenson, value judgments are characterized by their dynamic purpose. Prescriptive propositions are defined not by their descriptive meaning, but by their emotive meaning. Hence, normative discourse is distinguished by what it is <u>for</u>, or, more technically, by its perlocutionary force.

Prescriptivists agreed with this interpretation up to a point--normative discourse is not distinguished by its content. But then, we are told, neither can it be understood in terms of its perlocutionary force. On Hare's analysis, it can be <u>about</u> anything, or <u>for</u> any purpose.

Value judgments are characterized by their logical structure. Prescriptive propositions are defined by what they <u>do</u>; or better yet, by what <u>we do</u> conceptually in asserting them. Hence, normative discourse is distinguished by its illocutionary force.

Yet, we have examined prescriptivism and found it hardly more acceptable than intuitionism or emotivism. We might speculate that in each case the reason for failure can be traced to the assumption that values are

either purely objective or purely subjective.
Intuitionism assumes they are purely objective. Thus,
while our knowledge of values may rest on a certain mode
of perception (intuition or immediate apprehension),
values themselves exist independently of being known and
need not be perceived, by us or anyone else, in order
to partake of reality.

Emotivism and prescriptivism both assume that values
are purely subjective, that they are solely a matter of
volition, or a creation of the mind. Thus, in George
Berkeley's (1685-1753) famous phrase "essest percepi"
(literally, to be is to be perceived), the existence of
values consists in their being perceived. In short,
values are a function of perception, and for precisely
this reason their reality is contingent on their being
known.

Alternatives to these extremes must begin by
rejecting a hard and fast distinction between objective
and subjective reality. Dewey, for instance, proposed
a synthesis position that was rooted in a context of
action, a biological and social milieu in which
individuals deliberately do things and then must undergo
the consequences. By behaving purposefully they exercise
a creative influence, projecting their subjectivity in
a manner that helps define their environment.

However, by having to undergo the consequences they
are forced to face the objective facts of their practical
experience or "the world that is there." Dewey viewed
this as a transactional process and believed it to be
the source of all values. Thus understood, it is
synonymous with the process of valuation. If, as Dewey
maintained, it evolves a logic through experience, the
values articulated will eventually fall within the scope
of rationality, or as he preferred, "intelligence."

It should be obvious at once that taking this
proposal seriously requires us to reconsider the position
that Moore began by rejecting (see Chapter 4). To
conceive values in relation to their practical effects
is to think of them in terms of their natural properties.
This is exactly the position Moore believed he had
undermined with his "discovery" of the naturalistic
fallacy. In arguing that the meaning of normative
discourse is tied objectively to empirical facts, we shall
find ourselves in the end at the place where we originally
began.

DEFINITIONS OF VALUE
    How can the meaning of normative discourse be related
objectively to empirical facts? This is really a question
of definition that forces us to face up to Moore's
objection to "naturalism," to those theories of value,
or at least to those theories of moral value, "which
declare the sole good to consist in some one property
of things, which exists in time; and which do so because
they suppose that 'good' itself can be defined by
reference to such a property."[1] How can we define
values in terms of natural properties without committing
the naturalistic fallacy? In order to answer this
question we need to distinguish between formal and
substantive definitions.
    Formal definitions are those in which the term or
idea being defined (the definiendum) is impossible to
conceive apart from the terms or ideas which provide the
definition (the definiens). From a semantic viewpoint
the definiendum and the definiens are mutually
dependent, neither is intelligible independently of the
other.
    Substantive definitions are those in which the
definiendum and the definiens can be conceived
separately. Unlike formal definitions, they are not
tautologies in the strict sense. Both the term or idea
being defined and the terms or ideas providing the
definition remain essentially independent.
    Naturalistic conceptions of value have sometimes
been seen as formal definitions and sometimes as
substantive definitions. The naturalistic fallacy was
supposed to discredit both; formal definitions because
they are true but trivial, substantive definitions because
they violate "Hume's law," or the principle that "is"
statements never imply "ought" statements. Each of these
criticisms deserves closer study.

DEFLATING THE NATURALISTIC FALLACY
    If naturalistic conceptions of value were formal
definitions, they would be totally vacuous. The
definitional equation would be merely an identity

---

1. George Edward Moore, Principia Ethica (Cambridge,
    England: Cambridge Univ. Press, 1968), p. 41.

relationship and thus would not tell us anything new.
This is the reason Moore said that they argue in circles
or "beg the question." If the definiendum is normative,
so is the definiens. As an illustration, we might
imagine that "value" was defined formally as "that which
maximizes happiness." This being the case, "that which
maximizes happiness" would be inconceivable except as
having value. Knowing that some object or activity
maximized happiness, I could infer a priori that it had
value. Its having value would be part of its meaning.
As it stands the definition is an illusion. We understand
no more with it than without it. All it says, with
virtually no importance, is that whatever has value has
value.

Hence, the question is not whether formal definitions
of value are acceptable to reason, for clearly they are
not. Rather, the question is whether naturalistic
conceptions of value must be seen as formal definitions.
The answer is affirmative if the definiens incorporates
a judgment of value. To this degree the natural
properties that define value are themselves expressed
as values and the definitions become circular.

But perhaps this way of putting it is too strong.
For in one sense, almost if not all conceptions of natural
properties, and not just those we find in naturalistic
conceptions of value, require the making of value
judgments. Typically, naturalistic conceptions of value
rest on ideas about what benefits people, what they find
desirable or pleasant, what satisfies their needs or
serves their interests--in short, what contributes to
human welfare. These are matters that obviously involve
the exercise of normative judgment, judgment as to the
value or worth of things. But suppose we focused on ideas
about what people know, how much they have learned, or
how intelligent they are. Would not these too involve
the exercise of normative judgment? Even more concrete
notions, like running fast, being relaxed, and standing
firm, would seem to be subject to this requirement.

The reason is that natural properties are usually
if not always conceived as institutional facts and thus
presuppose standards. That standards are presupposed
does not mean they are not facts. They may require the
making of value judgments and still be empirically or
experientially based and conceived, independently of
having value. Why should it be different with natural
properties that define value?

Formal definitions are circular because the definiendum and the definiens cannot be separately conceived. They represent the same idea, even though it may be differently expressed. But with naturalistic conceptions of value there are at least two ideas, that of value itself and that of the natural property or properties which define value. Accordingly, the elements within the definition are conceptually distinct.

Thus, while naturalistic conceptions of value are based on conceptions of natural properties that involve the exercise of normative judgment, and while the reason for this is that these natural properties are conceived as institutional facts which, as a matter of logic, presuppose standards, the resultant definitions are not circular. The reason is that the standards presupposed are chiefly being used, not created or justified.

That standards are presupposed in conceptions of natural properties that define value is indisputable. But this does not render those conceptions normative. In truth, it renders them intelligible. Most if not all factual conceptions use standards to some degree. To avoid being normative it is enough that they not work primarily to create or justify these standards.

By presupposing standards rather than working primarily to create or justify them, the definiens in naturalistic conceptions of value can be conceived independently of the definiendum. To grant this concedes no more than what must be acknowledged about any institutional fact. As empirical or experientially based conceptions, they are logically distinct from the values they define. Hence, they function principally as factual judgments, not value judgments, and constitute what are essentially evaluations, not valuations.

When utilized in naturalistic conceptions of value, natural properties yield definitions that are substantive, not formal; definitions that are content-based, not that "beg the question." It is here where the argument Moore called "the open-question argument" comes into the picture. If naturalistic conceptions of value do not "beg the question" as formal definitions, do they not, as substantive definitions, violate "Hume's law"?

CONFRONTING THE IS/OUGHT DILEMMA
If values were defined substantively in terms of what benefits people, or contributes to human welfare,

we would find ourselves, as David Hume said, in something
of a philosophical predicament. In each instance, the
definiendum would tell us normatively what "ought" to
be the case, while the definiens would tell us
empirically what "is" the case. Must we not say, in the
light of the naturalistic fallacy, that this is logically
impossible? How can facts about what human beings find
desirable or pleasant, what satisfies their needs or
serves their interests, (assuming, of course, that these
are facts) imply what is right or good?

    Remember, we have two ideas here, not one. Each
can be separately conceived. Facts that can be conceived
independently of the values they define do not imply these
values, and descriptions about what benefits people or
contributes to human welfare do not entail prescriptions.
One can accept any evaluation and reject any valuation
not inherent in that evaluation without logical
inconsistency. Rationally we must repudiate any view
that equates, relates, or reduces values to that which
they are not. The gap between values and that which they
are not is logically insurmountable.

    But the opponents of naturalism want to say more
than this. In addition to saying that descriptions and
prescriptions are logically distinct, they also want to
say that descriptions and prescriptions are logically
unrelated. The former does not imply the latter, however.

    Granting that descriptions and prescriptions can
be conceived independently of each other, it does not
follow that they can be understood independently of
each other. By definition, facts are never conceived
as having value; that would always involve a second idea.
Thus, while as a matter of logic, we might accept or
reject any description as a criterion of merit, this does
not mean that our choice in one case would be as rational
as in the other.

    Rationality is nothing more than a capacity for
learning. To be rational is to engage in a process of
making sense out of nonsense. What is rational is
intelligible, what is not is absurd. That is to say,
rationality is a function of what is possible. We might
consider what is possible in any number of ways, but
basically it is a question of either what we can think
or imagine as an idea, or what we can perceive with our
senses as a fact.

    On the first standard, rationality is a function
of what is possible logically. If a proposition is

conceivable, it is rational. It is irrational or absurd
only if it violates established modes of communication,
only if it goes beyond the limits of language. The verbs
"can" and "must" have no limits other than logical limits.

To claim, for example, that the earth is filled with
raspberry jelly is perfectly consistent in itself and,
therefore, in itself is perfectly rational. But to claim,
in addition, that the earth's interior is a vacuum is
a logical contradiction. Unless the first claim is
abandoned the second is totally unthinkable and, hence,
totally irrational. But the truth remains that with
logical conceptions of rationality, reason is reducible
to technique. It focuses on how we think, not what.

On the second standard, rationality is a function
of what is possible experientially. A proposition is
rational if it is understandable in the light of our
dealings with nature. It is irrational or absurd if it
conflicts with the tested conclusions of common sense.
The verbs "can" and "must" are bounded by what is
empirically verifiable. To claim that the earth is filled
with raspberry jelly may be a perfectly well-formed
proposition, speaking logically. That is, in itself it
may be perfectly consistent. From the viewpoint of
experience, however, it is incomprehensible, it conflicts
with everything we know about the physical world. We
call it absurd not because it is a logical contradiction,
but because, as a matter of fact, it is ridiculous.
With experience as a basis for rationality, reason is
more than technique. It has as much to do with what
we think as how. It has as much to do with the
substance of our thought as with the form.

Whether rationality is conceived in logical or
experiential terms makes a great deal of difference when
trying to justify standards. In logical terms, standards
are rational so long as they display the right form.
Every logical option remains a rational option. They
could be about anything. Because logic provides no
substantive basis for choice, their content is
subjective. We could choose any standard and, assuming
we were clear and consistent, still be rationally
justified.

In experiential terms, things are quite the
contrary. Indeed, the traditional objection to any
experience based conception of rationality is that form
is lost in the insatiable currents of sensation. Dewey
tried to surmount this problem with his theory of

intelligence and his argument, rooted in his naturalism, that both the form and content of experience emerge as reality from a transactional process. But however this issue is viewed, experience defines standards substantively. If a standard cannot be seen within the limits of experience as contributing to human welfare, if empirically it is impossible, it is unintelligible as a standard.

This is not to say that the standard could not exist as a fact, or that the fact itself is unintelligible, only that it is unintelligible as a fact that might contribute to human welfare. To say within experience that a standard is unintelligible is not to say that the fact it depicts is empirically inconceivable, only that it is empirically inconceivable that the fact it depicts could be rationally justified as a standard, or as in any way leading to human betterment.

NATURALISM AS A THEORY OF VALUE

If the naturalistic fallacy is interpreted to mean that no one is ever logically obliged to accept any particular natural property as a criterion of merit, it would be correct but irrelevant to naturalism as a theory of value. It would say only that standards are built in logically to most if not all conceptions of natural properties and that these standards can always be rejected without logical inconsistency. But naturalism does not deny this. What it says is that standards cannot be understood except in terms of natural properties. And this, in turn, implies that standards must be defined substantively.

However, if the naturalistic fallacy is interpreted to mean not only that no one is ever logically obliged to accept any particular natural property as a criterion of merit, but that any particular natural property as a criterion of merit could always be rationally rejected, it obviously stands opposed to naturalism. The question is: Is it correct? Although any particular natural property as a criterion of merit could always be rejected without logical contradiction, in some cases rejection would be ridiculous. Just as some standards would be foolish to abide by, others would be silly to deny, despite what is possible logically.

In order to avoid confusion on this point we need to acknowledge a distinction between moral and nonmoral standards, or between "value" in the moral sense and "value" in the nonmoral sense. Economists speak of the value of a commodity without implying what is morally good, and mathematicians speak of the value of a variable without even so much as a human reference. In this nonmoral sense, standards are no more than facts, or more accurately, purported facts. They either exist or do not exist and need to be distinguished from those facts, or purported facts, which focus on human welfare and influence human conduct, facts, or purported facts, which as standards are either good or bad.

Unlike nominalistic theories of value, naturalism does not regard this distinction as arbitrary, or merely a question of logical form. If a standard can be demonstrated empirically to contribute to human welfare, it is rationally justifiable. If it can be demonstrated empirically to detract from human welfare, it is evil or wrong. To say this is not to say much, but it is to say something.[2] As Warnock contends:

> One could argue conclusively that some course of action would be, say, morally wrong if one could show that that course of action would lead quite certainly to certain consequences, which would constitute indisputably some serious harm to some innocent person or persons, and that there would accrue quite certainly no good to anyone which could possibly be held to outweigh those harmful consequences.[3]

Warnock gives as an example the case where a parent induces in his child an addiction to heroin. Surely, one could argue conclusively that this would be morally wrong. If it were put to someone who, while conceding the facts, denied that it was morally wrong, we could only say that this person "has not really followed the argument, or that he does not know what 'morally wrong' means."[4]

Unfortunately, most value questions cannot be answered with such finality. Our knowledge is limited

---

2. G. J. Warnock, Contemporary Moral Philosophy (New York: Macmillan, 1967), p. 67.
3. Ibid., p. 70.
4. Ibid., p. 70.

and our resources are far too few. But notice, the
arguments we formulate to defend our judgments are not
indecisive because of their formal properties, or because
they are not sufficiently "rigorous," but because of the
volatile and idiosyncratic nature of their subject matter.
If we understood more, we would disagree less. Knowledge
of fact gained through critical and reflective examination
of experience is the basis upon which this understanding
must rest.

Naturalism does not assume that arguments in defense
of values have the status of proofs. Not only does it
recognize that one substantive proposition never implies
another, but also that descriptive premises never imply
prescriptive conclusions. Not being known a priori,
prescriptions cannot be implied as conclusions in proofs.
They are warranted on the basis of evidence and share
the same epistemological status as statements of fact.
If statements of fact are acceptable as a knowledge
source, why not statements of value? Neither are any
the less compelling because logically they might be false.

That prescriptions are not usually ridiculous to
deny comes from their being, in comparison with
descriptions, extremely difficult to verify "beyond all
reasonable doubt." It is not, however, a result of their
inherent subjectivity. If nothing was known about what
people wanted or needed, if we had no idea of what was
in their interest, we might conclude that for them
anything whatsoever could have value.

But this conclusion, while in one sense perfectly
rational, speaks only to our ignorance and says nothing
about values per se, that is, nothing about their nature
or the conditions upon which they rest. Values, we have
said, are a function of human circumstances and these,
while obviously not improved by our lack of understanding,
do not lose their reality in being unknown.

We can agree with Dewey that the process of valuation
is not essentially subjective, but rather biological and
social.[5] It begins with desire. A desire is not merely
a mental state or a "wish." We can wish for something
without striving to bring it into actuality. Desire
produces physical tension and bodily movement so as to
satisfy an objective lack. While not itself a rational

5.   John Dewey, Theory of Valuation, International
      Encyclopedia of the Unified Sciences (Chicago: Univ.
      of Chicago Press, 1939), pp. 1-19.

standard, it initiates a process by which rational standards can be formed.

The sequence is one of moving from what is only felt or experienced as good, to what is felt or experienced as good as a result of rigorous and disciplined inquiry, or alternatively, as a result of "intelligent practical action." What is enjoyed prior to intelligent practical action is thus transformed and, when valued rationally, becomes what is enjoyed as a consequence of intelligent practical action. What begins as desire ends as enlightened conduct, or as what is truly desirable.

Rational standards are desirable standards. The good is derived from thoughtful action motivated by desires in a problematic situation, a situation we find, practically speaking, unworkable. What is desirable is a fact as well as a value, and to this extent it cannot be expressed in formal or logical propositions. It exists objectively within the frame of experience, and is known as a product of an intelligent conversation with nature. In Dewey's words:

> Examination of the situation in respect to the conditions that constitute lack and need and thus serve as positive means for formation of an attainable end or outcome, is the method by which warranted (required and effective) desires and ends-in-view are formed: by which, in short, valuation takes place.[6]

Dewey felt especially strong about the relationship of ends and means in this situation.

> the relational character of the things that are employed as means does not prevent the things from having their own immediate qualities. . . . There is nothing in the nature of prizing or desiring to prevent their being directed to things which are means, and there is nothing in the nature of means to militate against their being desired and prized. . . . [A]ny theory which isolates valuation of ends from appraisal of means equates the spoiled child and the irresponsible adult to the mature and sane person.[7]

---

6. Ibid., p. 55.
7. Ibid., pp. 27, 31.

Having knowledge of what is desirable in practical affairs, in this full and total sense, is the rational equivalent of possessing justifiable human values.

If the philosophical skeptic protests that, after all, this knowledge is based on experience and that, therefore, it is not infallible, he gives us on one interpretation wise and sensitive counsel. For not only are human beings diverse and difficult to understand, but to one degree or another their world is constantly in flux. Continually, we are forced to rethink our opinions. Reflection is never over and done with, finished for all time. But if the skeptic means, additionally, that questions of value preclude reason, that in their content if not in their form reason demands that we withhold commitment, his advice is neither responsible nor prudent.

Circumstances will often force us to decide on questions of value without having sufficient or adequate knowledge. All we can do is make the best of what we have--and hope. But our efforts can have their benefits. Not only might we be right, but in the very process of acting we have the means for gaining new knowledge, so that next time we will be better prepared to act intelligently.

I N D E X

Anscombe, G. E. M., 31
  "On Brute Facts" (1958),
    31 n
A priori, 18, 41, 69, 78,
    84
  "a priori process," 44
  "synthetic-a priori
    truths," 44
Arguments
  "deductive," 17
  demonstrative, 15-16
  explanations, 16, 18-21
  justifications, 16-17,
    21-26
  moral, 56
  normative, 39
  premise-conclusion, 13-14
  proofs, 16, 17-18
Attitudes, 54, 60
  and feelings, 57-62
  C. L. Stevenson on, 53-54
  J. O. Urmson on, 57-60
Austin, J. L., How to Do
    Things with Words
    (1965), 64 n
  prescriptivism and work
    of, 63-65
Ayer, A. J., 38
  Language, Truth and Logic
    (1952), 51, 52 n

on prescriptive propo-
    sitions, 51-52

Belief, 60
  C. L. Stevenson on,
    53-54
  J. O. Urmson on, 59
Berkeley, George, "essest
    percepi," 76
Brute facts, 31-33
  defined, 31
Butler, Bishop Joseph, 43

Carnap, Rudolph, Philos-
    ophy and Logical
    Syntax (1935), 51,
    51 n
  on value statements, 51
Conduct, influence of
    values on, 47, 55,
    56-57
Constitutive rules
  classified as prescrip-
    tive, 35-36
  defined, 34

Definiendum, defined, 77
Definiens, defined, 77
Demonstrative arguments,
    15-16

Descriptions, 27, 28, 80,
    84
  linguistic function,
    27-28, 30
Descriptive meaning, 55,
    75
Descriptive propositions,
    27-36
  classifying, 28, 32, 35
  as distinct from "is"
    statements, 28-30
  linguistic function, 27-
    28, 30
  as related to institu-
    tional facts, 31-33
Descriptivism, 27
Dewey, John, 19, 30-31,
    34 n, 38, 60-61, 76,
    84-85
  "Ethical Subject-Matter
    and Language" (1945),
    61 n
  on intelligence, 76, 81-82
  on reality, 81-82
  Theory of Valuation
    (1939), 31 n, 84 n,
    85 n
  on transaction and values,
    76
  on valuation, 84

Education, as human institu-
    tion, 9-10
Educational theories, 9-12
  as answering important
    questions, 10
  as distinguished by
    subject matter, 9-10
  as providing under-
    standing, 10-12
Emotive influence, 61-62
Emotive meaning, 55, 61, 75
Emotivism, 52, 56, 57, 62,
    65, 68, 70, 75
  and A. J. Ayer, 51-52
  and Rudolf Carnap, 51

  criticisms of, 56-62
  defined, 49-50
  and C. K. Ogden, 50-51
  and prescriptive propo-
    sitions, 64
  reasoning of, 50
  and I. A. Richards, 50-
    51
  and C. L. Stevenson, 52-
    56
Emotivists, 22, 38, 60,
    61, 63
Empiricism (philosoph-
    ical), 7, 41-42
  rise of, 18, 41
Epistemic relationship
    between premise and
    conclusion, 14
Evaluations, 30, 38, 79,
    80
Existentialists, 38
Experience, 18
  constructed sym-
    bolically, 4
  learn from, 4
  C. S. Peirce on, 23
  theory organizes, 10
Explanations, 16, 18-21
  and relationships
    between facts, 21

"Fallibilism," 23
Feelings, and attitudes,
    58-60
Flew, A. G. N., 38
  "On Not Deriving 'Ought'
    from 'Is'" (1969),
    38 n
Formal definitions, 77
  of value, 77-79
Formalism, 39, 41, 42, 49,
    50

Green, Thomas, The Activi-
    ties of Teaching
    (1971), 25 n

on justification, 24-25

Hare, R. M., 38, 66, 67,
    68-69, 71, 75
    Freedom and Reason
        (1963), 65, 66 n,
        67 n
    The Language of Morals
        (1952), 65, 66 n
    on normative discourse,
        65-67
    on prescribing, 68-69
    "Review of Warnock's
        Contemporary Moral
        Philosophy" (1968),
        68 n
Hartshorne, Charles, ed.,
    Collected Papers of
    Charles Sanders Peirce
    (1965), 24 n
Hudson, W. D., ed., The Is-
    Ought Question (1969),
    38 n
Hume, David, 38, 80
    "Hume's Law," 77, 79

Ideas
    abstract, 4
    and proofs, 21
Illocutionary acts, 63-66
    defined, 63-64
    and meaningful proposi-
        tions, 64
Imperatives, 65, 66, 69
    categorical, 67
    hypothetical, 67
Institutional facts, 33-36,
    78, 79
    defined, 31-32
    and descriptive proposi-
        tions, 32
    essence of, 32
Instrumentalism, 5-9
    and the creative
        dimension, 8
    and empiricism, 7

Abraham Kaplan on, 7
    view of knowledge, 6
    Grover Maxwell on, 6-7
    and positivism, 9
    and realism, 6
Intuition, 42, 44, 76
Intuitionism, 49, 56, 64,
    70, 75, 76
    criticisms of, 45-48
    defined, 42
    G. E. Moore on, 42-44
    and nonnatural proper-
        ties, 43, 49
    and prescriptive propo-
        sitions, 46

Judgments, 24-25, 71
    defined, 24
    of facts, 29-30, 45, 67
    of value, 11, 12, 29,
        30-31, 36, 39, 45,
        63, 67, 71, 75
Justifications, 16, 36,
    66-67
    as arguments, 13-16
    and certainty, 11
    conclusions of, 13-14
    as eternal verities, 22
    logic of, 21-26
    premises of, 13-14
    and standards, 37
    validity of, 13-14

Kant, Immanuel, 44, 67
Kaplan, Abraham, 4, 5, 7,
    8, 9, 19, 61-62
    The Conduct of Inquiry
        (1964), 5 n, 6 n,
        7 n, 8 n, 9 n, 19 n
    "Logical Empiricism and
        Value Judgments"
        (1963), 62 n
Kennedy, Gail, "The Prag-
    matic Naturalism of
    Chauncey Wright"
    (1935), 6 n

Kingsley, Charles, 39

Language, 29, 30, 50, 55,
    63
Locutionary acts, 63-64
    defined, 63-64

Maxwell, Grover, 6-7
    "The Ontological Status
        of Theoretical
        Entities" (1962), 7 n
Mead, G. H., The Philosophy
    of the Act (1938), 21 n
Miller, David L., George
    Herbert Mead--Self,
    Language, and the World
    (1973), 21 n
Moore, G. E., 42-44, 45-46,
    50, 55, 57
    and "the naturalistic
        fallacy," 43, 76-82
    objection to "naturalism,"
        77
    Principia Ethica (1903),
        42, 42 n, 77 n
    and a referential theory
        of meaning, 54-55
    self-evident values, 44
Morris, Charles W., ed.,
    The Philosophy of the
    Act (1938), 21 n

Naturalism, 27, 77, 80, 82,
    84
    and formal definitions,
        77-79
    and nominalistic theories
        of value, 83
    and substantive defini-
        tions, 79-82
    as a theory of value,
        82-86
Nominalism, 39
    and abstractions, 49

Ogden, C. K.

on ethics, 50-51
    The Meaning of Meaning
    (1923), 50, 51 n
Ontology, and formal
    logic, 18
Ontological significance
    of explanations, 20
    of formal propositions,
        18
    of justifications, 22

Peirce, Charles S.
    Collected Papers of
        Charles Sanders
        Peirce (1965)
        (Hartshorne and
        Weiss, eds.), 24 n
    on experience, 24
    and "fallibilism," 23
Perlocutionary acts, 66
    defined, 63-64
Perlocutionary force
    and normative discourse,
        75
    and normative pronounce-
        ments, 65
Phenomenalists, 38
Positivism
    and instrumentalism, 9
    and Realists, 7-8
Positivistic principle of
    meaning, 50
Positivists, 4
Prescribing, defined,
    68-69
Prescriptions, 28, 80, 84
    linguistic functions,
        27-28, 30
    related to descriptions,
        80
Prescriptive propositions,
    27, 28, 31, 33, 36,
    37, 38, 46, 64, 66,
    67, 70, 71, 75
    A. J. Ayer on, 51-52
    classifying, 28, 32, 35

as distinct from "ought"
  statements, 28-30
linguistic functions,
  27-28, 30
as related to behavior, 68
Prescriptivism, 62, 63, 65,
  68, 69, 70, 71, 72, 73,
  75-76
and J. L. Austin, 63-65
criticisms of, 68-70
and nominalism, 65-68
and rationality, 70-73
G. J. Warnock on, 69, 70,
  71, 72, 73
Proofs, 16, 17-18

Rationalism (philosophical),
  decline of, 18
Rationalists (continental),
  7
Rationality, 78, 80
as a function of what is
  possible experi-
  entially, 81
as a function of what is
  possible logically,
  80-81
and intelligence, 76,
  81-82
as a logical stipulation,
  70-73
and naturalism as a theory
  of value, 82-86
as technical, 9
Realism
and Francis Bacon, 7
and inquiry, 5-8
Abraham Kaplan on, 5
Grover Maxwell on, 6-7
Reflection, 86
Regulative rules
classified as descriptive,
  35
defined, 34
Richards, I. A.
on ethics, 50-51

The Meaning of Meaning
  (1923), 50, 51 n

Science, rise of, 41
Searle, John R., 38
"Deriving 'Ought' from
  'Is'" (1969), 31 n
on descriptive and
  prescriptive propo-
  sitions, 36-38
Skeptic (philosophical),
  86
Soundness (of arguments),
  defined, 16
Standards, 27, 30, 33-34
and constitutive rules,
  35-36
rationality in creating,
  38-40, 79-86
and regulative rules,
  35
use in arguments, 37
Stevenson, C. L., 38,
  52-56, 57, 58, 60,
  68, 71, 75
on attitudes, 53-54
on beliefs, 53-54
"The Emotive Meaning of
  Ethical Terms"
  (1963), 54 n
on ethical disagreement,
  53-54
Ethics and Language
  (1944), 52, 53 n,
  54 n, 57
Facts and Values--
  Studies in Ethical
  Analysis (1963),
  53 n, 54 n
"On the Nature of
  Ethical Disagree-
  ment" (1963), 53 n,
  54 n
Substantive definitions,
  77
of value, 77, 79-82

Theory
  as complete, 10
  as credible, 11
  as distinguished in
    education, 9-12
  genesis of, 3-4
  as an idea, 4-5
  and instrumentalism, 5, 6,
    7-9
  and realism, 5, 6-7
  soundness of, 10
  subject matter of, 10, 47

Urmson, J. O., 57-60
  The Emotive Theory of
    Ethics (1969), 58 n,
    59 n, 60 n

Validity
  defined, 14
  demonstrations of, 14-15
  and soundness, 16
  types of, 16-17
Valuation, 31 n, 34, 73, 76,
    79, 84-85, 84 n, 85 n
Values, 11-12, 26, 73-74,
    76, 77
  classical view of, 41-42
  and descriptive proposi-
    tions, 30
  disputes over, 53, 54
  and dynamic use of
    language, 54-55
  and emotivism, 50-56
  and facts, 38-40
  and formal definitions,
    77-79
  and formalism, 49

  as instrumental, 30
  and intuitionism, 42-48,
    56
  as justifiable, 86
  moral and nonmoral,
    82-83
  and naturalism, 82-86
  and prescriptive propo-
    sitions, 30-31
  and prescriptivism, 63
  as self-evident, 44
  as social conventions,
    31
  and substantive defini-
    tions, 79-82
Vienna Circle, 38, 51

Warnock, G. J., 39, 45,
    46, 47, 48, 56, 57,
    60, 61, 69, 70, 71,
    72, 73, 83
  Contemporary Moral
    Philosophy (1967),
    39 n, 42 n, 45 n,
    46 n, 47 n, 48 n,
    57 n, 60 n, 61 n,
    66 n, 69 n, 70 n,
    71 n, 72 n, 73 n,
    83 n
Weiss, Paul, ed.,
    Collected Papers of
    Charles Sanders
    Peirce (1965), 24 n
Wright, Chauncey, 6
  Gail Kennedy, "The Prag-
    matic Naturalism of
    Chauncey Wright,"
    6 n